STUDIES IN HISTORY, ECONOMICS AND PUBLIC LAW

Edited by the

FACULTY OF POLITICAL SCIENCE
OF COLUMBIA UNIVERSITY

NUMBER 400

EXPERIMENTS IN CREDIT CONTROL
THE FEDERAL RESERVE SYSTEM

BY

CAROLINE WHITNEY

EXPERIMENTS IN CREDIT CONTROL
THE FEDERAL RESERVE SYSTEM

BY

CAROLINE WHITNEY, PH.D.

NEW YORK

COLUMBIA UNIVERSITY PRESS

LONDON: P. S. KING & SON, LTD.

1934

PRINTED IN THE UNITED STATES OF AMERICA

TO

MARIAN PARKER WHITNEY

PROFESSOR EMERITUS

OF

VASSAR COLLEGE

whose independence of thought and activity
have marked a path

PREFACE

THE world depression of industry and trade which commenced in 1929 brought with it the greatest banking collapse in the history of the United States. At the time when all banks of the country were closed during the opening days of the political administration known as the " New Deal, " much criticism was heard from laymen of the inconsiderate bank depositors, who had asked their banks to do what they had always promised to do—to convert deposits into note obligations of the United States Government. Some even expressed sympathy with unfortunate bankers whose assets had depreciated due to what they considered to be the inevitable action of economic forces. In this mass movement of sympathy for bankers two important facts were consistently overlooked. First, when state or city banking holidays had been in force, some individual institutions had been able to remain open and to meet all demands upon them. Second, with the exception of the two countries most impoverished by the effects of the Treaty of Versailles, no country of the world, no matter how small, had witnessed a tying-up of all of its banking operations in the course of the depression.

At the time of the passage of the Federal Reserve Act the idea became current that the bank failures which had characterized American financial history would be relegated to the archives of history. This idea was so persistent that it permeated college text books on Economics, even those which were written years after the Federal Reserve System had begun operations. In spite of this hope, bank failures have been more frequent under the Federal Reserve System—even during the heyday of the " New Era "—than under the previous system of inelastic banking.

It seems apparent to any student of the subject that the fault lies, not with the depression, but with the banking process and the influence upon it of the operations of the Federal Reserve banks. Certain " New Era " practices put the banks in a position where they could not function if business conditions underwent any changes.

Due to the fact that the faults of our banking system were traceable to events which took place before 1929, this book concerns itself primarily with the decade following the close of the World War, tracing the effects of policies pursued during this decade in the subsequent four years. Those banking policies which were under the control of the Federal Reserve banks were to some extent avoidable, and therefore should be studied in detail. A new plan of action by which the Federal Reserve System may influence banks and bankers to practice more sound methods in their own field will be presented. The fact that the pursuance of such a policy would result in smaller banking operations should not be viewed with alarm, for any loss to American pride in the form of small size will be amply compensated by high quality.

Academic advisors to the Federal Reserve System and to the United States Treasury have hoped that the actions of the Federal Reserve banks might influence the course of business and prices. In cases where the effects of given policies are uncertain, they have recommended a course of experimentation. But the possible deleterious effects of experiments, whose effects cannot be accurately forseen, have been overlooked. The continuation of such recommendations makes imperative a study of the actual effects of currency and banking experiments.

The author wishes to express indebtedness to the following members of the Faculties of Business and Political Science of Columbia University, who have assisted at various stages of the preparation of this manuscript: Professor H. Parker

Willis, Professor John M. Chapman, Professor James W. Angell, Mr. Arthur Burns and Professor B. Haggott Beckhart; also to Professor Simon S. Kuznets of the University of Pennsylvania. The members of the Banking Seminar of Columbia University, conducted by Professor Willis, have rendered much helpful criticism. Doctor Margaret G. Myers, Mrs. Helen Slade and Doctor Horace B. Davis have assisted by criticizing the manuscript.

Chapter III is an abridgment of a Chapter by the author in *The Banking Outlook* by H. Parker Willis and John M. Chapman, Columbia University Press, N. Y., 1934. It is included by permission of the publisher.

LIST OF CHARTS

TABLE OF CONTENTS

CHAPTER IV

Federal Reserve Policy and the Commercial Credit System

CHAPTER V

The Bankers' Acceptance Market

CHAPTER VI

Brokers' Loans and Federal Reserve Policy

CHAPTER VII

Federal Reserve Policy and Rates of Interest

CHAPTER VIII

Interest Rates and the Flow of Credit

CHAPTER IX

Federal Reserve Policy and the Problem of Liquidity

CHAPTER I

The Function Of The Federal Reserve System

FUNCTIONS OF CENTRAL BANKS

Central banks are identified with several activities not always practiced by business banks. They also compete with business banks in other fields. Practices in different countries vary first with the constitutions of their central banks and second with local banking practices. But there are some functions which these institutions always perform besides other duties which devolve upon them in countries which possess complicated financial systems.

Central banks issue circulating notes. In most countries they possess a monopoly of note issue or else the privilege of issuing all but a small and limited portion of the notes in circulation. This authority gives them power to dictate terms to banks which are in need of notes for deposit conversion.

Foreign exchange dealings are within the province of central banking activity, for these institutions are charged with the responsibility of maintaining the gold reserves of their countries intact. Their reserves of precious metals are fixed by law. In order to be able to vary their credit extensions with the needs of borrowers, they must have some means of maintaining their own reserves within the legal limits. In addition to their own reserves, the central banks of the more advanced countries hold the reserves of business banks. In such countries central banks are responsible for all metallic reserves of banks. But to control gold movements central banks depend in normal times upon control of rates of interest, which are assumed to determine the direction of gold movements. It is only in times of stress that they take control of the foreign exchange markets.

Central banks are generally the chief agencies of government finance. In performing this function good practice requires that they give their governments no preferential treatment over business customers; in fact that they give preference to their other clients. This canon of central banking practice is more frequently violated than any other canon. Lending to the government may be combined with lending to business, but when the former type of credit accommodation is large inflation results.

In countries in which there are well established money markets, the central banks assume control of these markets. This control is chiefly expressed in terms of the influence which the operations of the central bank have upon the rate charged for discount accommodation. The power to alter rates is exercised through different means according to the type of money market in existence in the country concerned. In England the Bank competes with the joint stock banks in discounting acceptances for bill brokers, who represent the core of the open money market. The Bank enters the market at times when money is tight and joint stock banks refuse to lend, thus making the market rate conform to its rate. In times of easy money, the Bank in not in the bill market and the joint stock banks determine rates. An artificial stimulus to contract is brought about by having the Bank sell its holdings of government bonds in the market, causing the joint stock banks to cease lending and the bill brokers to apply at the Bank. The Bank, therefore, also competes with the market as an investor in governmental consols.

The nonexistence of a discount market in the United States made the organization of the Federal Reserve System take a different form than that of the central banks of

Europe. Since the American money market consists for the most part of a number of markets for customer loans at the thousands of banks scattered throughout the country and of a well developed open market for securities and for security loans in New York City, and since it was desired that the Federal Reserve System ignore the latter in an effort to discourage its further growth, the Reserve banks were set up as regional central banks to supervise the commercial banks directly. It was hoped that the operations of the regional Reserve banks would have some effect upon rates charged customers and lending practices at banks in their districts. But the so-called market for customer loans at banks does not partake of the nature of a money market for most borrowers have no alternative but to borrow at one bank and the element of competition is absent in rate determination. The competitive money markets in the United States, besides the above mentioned security markets and their adjuncts, the security loan markets, consist of those large commercial borrowers who have the option of borrowing at any one of a number of banks or who may borrow by selling notes to note brokers or else at banks. The sphere of influence of the Federal Reserve System is therefore this small competitive part of the customer loan market as well as a market which had previously not existed—the discount market for bankers' acceptances.

The Federal Reserve banks deal extensively in the market for government bonds as well as in commercial loan markets. These dealings were permitted in order to give the Reserve System a means of exercising leadership over the commercial money markets, as the Bank of England does through its dealings in consols. But the close relationship of the Federal Reserve System to the Federal Government has caused these dealings to increase very greatly as time went on. At the same time the fiction is maintained that the dealings in government bonds are undertaken purely to influence the volume of credit going to business.

CREDIT, MONEY AND RESERVES

Credit, that vague term representing the basis of future transactions of all sorts, is today one part of most exchanges. In credit transactions one party gives goods, or the means of obtaining them, while the other party gives a promise to return a given amount of purchasing power at a specified date in the future. The basis of this promise, which leads it to be acceptable to those who take it in trade, is the credit of the purchaser or borrower. Credit is an asset of individuals offering credit instruments in exchange for goods which may be pledged as a guarantee of repayment. The lender or seller is said to extend credit. Actually he extends goods or purchasing power, by recognizing credit.

There are two types of credit transaction: those in the form of purchases and those in the form of loans. Bank credit arises in the case of the second type only. In the former case, the seller accepts a promise to pay in return for useful goods. In the latter case, the borrower gives a promise to pay in the future and receives the promise of the lender to pay in the present. With the promise of the lender, he may purchase goods. Banks' promises to pay enjoy a wide circulation and so credit transactions at banks are frequent, although they are always anticipatory to transactions in goods. Where borrowers exchange the promises of their customers to pay in the future for bank promises to pay in the present, known as discounts, the credit transaction appears to be subsequent to the transaction in goods, but this is not actually the case, for the bank borrowing would not have taken place, had the borrower not wished to purchase more goods.

In cases of bank borrowing the lender offers a promise to pay backed by his credit. The bank does not create credit but creates a liability against itself, which circulates due to the fact that the bank has credit. Where, then, does the credit of society arise? It arises from the future surplus earnings of business firms and individuals. The credit of banks is a reflection of the credit of those to whom they have extended purchasing power and therefore is not counted as a part of credit of society to avoid duplication. The volume of credit in existence at any time is a fixed amount. Of 90-day credit, there is the present value of the total profit of undertakings and savings of individuals 90 days hence. Of 120-day credit there is another sum. Factors entering into the economic system between now and the maturity of any of this credit recognized may alter these sums, but at the moment they stand as they are. For example, at the end of 30 days there may be more 60-day credit than there is 90-day credit now. But this does not alter the present situation.

Banks, by their actions, cannot increase or diminish the volume of credit but they can recognize more or less credit, thus altering the volume of the circulating medium. They maintain their own credit, which enables their liabilities to circulate as purchasing power, by recognizing valid claims to credit so that it is known that the liabilities of the banks will be exchangeable into goods or into money in the future.

Money is an asset of society and circulates against goods along with credit. In some cases it is useful as a substitute for credit, as in settling unpaid international balances or balances between banks. In the United States, money takes several forms: demand liabilities of the Treasury, known as currency, and balances at Federal Reserve banks. The first is used to settle international balances, the second to settle debts with those who have no bank accounts and the third to settle unpaid balances of banks with each other. In practice the only kind of money which did not arise out of some sort of a credit transaction is gold. Currency issued by the Treasury or made payable at the Treasury, as is the case with bank notes, originates in the credit of the government. Federal Reserve bank balances originate in the credit of the Federal Reserve banks. But these forms of money may be used along with newly recognized bank credit to pay for goods.

Banks which create liabilities against credit which does not exist, this type of credit being known as illiquid credit, gradually lose their currency and Reserve balances and become insolvent. But those recognizing only valid claims to credit, find their reserves of currency or Reserve bank balances replenished from time to time as loans mature and are repaid. But they must maintain reserves for the possible creation of liabilities and the maturities of loans. The extent of reserves required depends upon the nature of the businesses acquiring the rights to use the bank's liabilities. No automatic rule of reserves is possible, although the rough rule embodied in the National Banking Act and carried over into the Federal Reserve Act, that reserves must be larger for banks in large places than for banks in small places, is an embodiment of this principle.

Banks do not like to withdraw their reserves for fear of the effect which such a practice would have upon their credit standing and because they are not allowed to do so. Therefore, the lawful reserves of banks are actually used in cases of liquidation only. But banks maintain an additional reserve in the form of currency or of assets which are shiftable to other banks in exchange for immediately available purchasing power. In order to insure that the shift may take place there must be a group of banks which are unusually strong at all times. The duty has devolved upon the Reserve banks of providing a place to which such assets can always be shifted.

THE FUNCTIONS OF THE RESERVE BANKS

From the previous discussion it is evident that the Reserve banks may have a function in maintaining their liquidity for emergencies and in watching the liquidity of their members as well as their solvency, or reserve positions. At times when member banks appear to be recognizing illiquid credit, the Reserve banks should limit their accomodations to them. But the Reserve banks have no power to alter the volume of credit in existence awaiting recognition. If they extend more Reserve bank credit to the market, they may increase the reserves of banks, but they do not alter the real basis of credit —the future surplus of production over consumption of the individuals making up society. The Reserve banks should also be in a position to assist banks which are liquid to remain solvent during the intervals between the recognition of credit and the repayment of loans.

The Federal Reserve Act was enacted into law in order to provide an elastic currency, elastic bank reserves and a discount market.[1] The meaning of these terms must be kept clearly in mind in determining the extent to which Federal Reserve policy has been effective.

The meaning of elastic is given in Webster's dictionary as "enlarging or decreasing readily in response to a change in stimulus." In other words, an elastic currency enlarges in volume when the public shows a desire to convert bank deposits into currency and equally readily diminishes when not needed. An elastic bank reserve increases when banks increase their liabilities through credit recognition and decreases when the liabilities are extinguished by repayment.

[1] The first two reasons were given by Senator Glass of Virginia, one of the founders of the System, as the chief reasons for the existence of a Federal Reserve System. See *Speech of Hon. Carter Glass in the Senate of the United States*, Mon. and Tues., Jan. 16 and 17, 1922. The third reason was emphasized by Paul M. Warburg, *The Federal Reserve System*, N. Y., 1930, vol. I.

Thus, bank reserves should be related to the volume of credit in existence. The Federal Reserve Act supplied an elastic currency and elastic bank reserves by defining as currency or bank reserves any credit recognized by Reserve banks. It linked the rate of recognition of this credit with the volume of credit in existence by making the Reserve banks willing to recognize any credit which possessed a very high degree of liquidity. But the closeness of the Federal Reserve System to the government made the framers of the Federal Reserve Act include in liquid credit government credit of all sorts, and much government credit is illiquid. Consequently, the Federal Reserve System became a tool for inflation—or the recognition of illiquid credit.

The establishment of a discount market was inserted to render secondary reserves of banks convertible into cash by being shifted to banks which have more currency on hand. This was accomplished by the authorization of the right to create bankers' acceptances, which had been shown by experience to be the most shiftable bank assets in London, and by the creation of a market for these credit instruments at the Reserve banks. Safeguards were set up to insure that these instruments would be liquid as well as shiftable in order that the Reserve banks would not lose liquidity at times when they were forced to serve as a market for bankers' acceptances. How these rules were made and later relaxed will be the subject of a chapter of this study.

SUMMARY

The money markets in the United States consist largely of security markets and their adjuncts, security loan markets, and the many markets for customer loans at banks. The Federal Reserve System did not wish to deal in the former markets, with the exception of the market for government bonds, and therefore was organized to control whatever competitive elements there are in the remainder of the money market. These are those markets where borrowers may have more than one source of loans and the newly organized discount market for bankers' acceptances.

The intended functions of the Federal Reserve System were to provide an elastic currency and a system of elastic bank reserves and to establish a discount market. Elasticity involves the regulation of the volume of currency and bank reserves to fit the credit needs of society. Since credit is an asset of the individuals making up society and cannot be manufactured by banks the powers of the Federal Reserve System to alter the volume of credit are limited. But the recognition of credit which does not exist is a cause of the depletion of bank reserves and should be the sign for the initiation of a policy of restriction by the Federal Reserve System.

CHAPTER II

The Mechanism of Credit Control

THE MECHANISM OF CREDIT CONTROL

The Reserve banks attempt to control the rate of credit recognition by commercial banks by three means. The first is by alterations in market rates of interest—that is, by rates charged to ultimate borrowers from banks. It is hoped that high rates will act to curtail the desire to borrow while low rates will stimulate it. This may be called " indirect control " as it is exercised through the channel of interest rates, the assumption being made that interest rates affect the rate of borrowing.

The second method of credit control is more direct. The Reserve banks attempt to alter the reserve positions of banks in order to encourage or discourage them to recognize applications for loans. The theory underlying an artificial increase in bank reserves as a stimulus to lending is that the banks may be refusing applications from clients possessing credit due to their reserve positions. If this be the case, the reserve positions of banks have suffered either due to previous extensions of illiquid credit or to short period losses pending the maturity of outstanding good loans. In the former instance, there is no guarantee that the new reserves may not be used for further illiquid credit extensions and so the practice is dangerous. But in the latter instance, bank reserves as a whole will not have suffered. The extension of new Reserve bank credit must take place at certain points so that it will be availed of by those banks which need reserves pending the repayment of liquid loans. The theory underlying a decrease in bank reserves as a deterrent to borrowing is that since banks are expanding their liabilities at too fast a rate, any artificial reduction in their reserves will be followed by more refusals to extend credit.

The Reserve banks likewise hope to improve the quality of credit, rendering it more liquid, by the indirect inducement to banks to make loans in a form which will be eligible for obtaining additional advances from their Reserve banks.

THE TOOLS OF CONTROL

The Federal Reserve System has various methods of influencing the volume of credit extended, the cost of credit extension and the form which credit instruments take. The more important of these are:

(1) changes in the rates charged by Reserve banks on various kinds of paper—the rediscount rate and the buying rate for bankers' acceptances purchased in the open market;

(2) changes in the holdings of Reserve banks of earning assets purchased in the open market;

(3) so-called "moral suasion" or the refusal to rediscount paper for member banks which do not follow the policies of the Federal Reserve System in their loan policies;

(4) changes in the eligibility and acceptability requirements for paper rediscounted at or sold to Reserve banks.

There are also other instruments of control which have been used but little.

Discount Rates

Rate control is exercised through two channels. The first comprises changes in the rate of discount charged by each Reserve bank on paper offered to it by member banks which wish to borrow. These changes are made by the Board of Directors of the local Reserve bank but are subject to review and determination by the Federal Reserve Board.

It has not yet been settled whether the Board has the right to force changes in rates upon unwilling Reserve banks. In one case the Board assumed this power. In August, 1927, when the Federal Reserve Board ordered the Federal Reserve Bank of Chicago to lower its rate from 4 percent to 3½ percent, the Chicago Bank, feeling that this move would unduly encourage speculation, refused to do so. After a month taken up with negotiations, the Bank gave in and followed the orders of the Board. But this case was not considered to be a precedent as it was informally conceded that the Board would never again bring such pressure to bear upon an unwilling Federal Reserve bank.[1]

In general, the procedure leading up to a change in the rediscount rate at any Reserve bank is approximately as follows. At its reguar weekly meeting the Board of Directors of the Reserve bank decides whether the rate in effect shall continue. If it decides against a change in rate no action is taken but the Federal Reserve Board is notified immediately of the fact. If it decides to change the rate, the Reserve bank communicates with the Federal Reserve Board by telephone and receives notice of the confirmation or otherwise. If the action is not confirmed no announcement is made, although the facts frequently leak out to the press. In the case of the Federal Reserve Bank of New York action was taken to raise its rate from 5 percent to 6 percent at frequent intervals on and after February 14, 1929, but this action was not approved by the Federal Reserve Board until August 9th. If the rate action is confirmed the news is immediately given out to the press, which features it prominently in its news columns, for the community attaches great importance to discount rate changes.

[1] A description of the events and negotiations preceding this exercise of power is given in an article by J. M. Daiger, "Did the Federal Reserve Play Politics?", *Current History*, October, 1932, pp. 25-32.

Reasons for rate changes are never formally announced. The excuse given by Federal Reserve officials for this omission is that the reasons are so many and various that no one cause can be assigned for each action. We now have a record of the things which the Reserve banks hoped to accomplish by changes in their rediscount rate policy from their answers to a questionnaire sent to them by a subcommittee of the Committee on Banking and Currency of the United States Senate in 1931.[2] In answer to a question relative to the more important considerations leading to changes in rates of rediscount the Reserve banks gave the following reasons for both increases and reductions in rates: (1) a previous increase or decrease in open market rates of interest; (2) to bring the policy of the individual Reserve bank in question into line with the policies of the other Reserve banks; (3) to check an increase or decrease in member bank borrowings; (4) to bring the nation's credit supplies into line with the nation's business needs. Reasons for rate increases alone also included a desire to check security speculation and to force a seasonal liquidation of credit. Reasons for rate reductions other than those given above were to attract member bank borrowings away from commercial banks in larger centers, to check a decline in business, employment and commodity prices, and to repel gold imports thus stabilizing international money markets. This summary shows that the Reserve banks hoped for many things as a result of changes in their discount rates. But the frequent rate changes dictated by a desire to make the discount rate conform to open market rates or to attract member bank borrowings away from commercial banks indicate that the Reserve banks were not exerting leadership over the money market but rather following it.

[2] *Hearings before a Sub-Committee of the Committee on Banking and Currency of the United States Senate, 71st.. Congress, 3rd. Session, 1931, Pursuant to S. Res. 71*, appendix, part 6, pp. 748-793.

The extent to which their aims were realized may be gleaned from their answers to the next question. Three Reserve banks—Cleveland, Minneapolis and Richmond—were quite well satisfied with the results of their action, although it may be noted that these are interior Reserve banks and, therefore, ones whose hopes were necessarily modest. The nine remaining Reserve banks were not content with the results of their efforts to check security speculation in 1928 and 1929 by means of the discount rate, although they were not dissatisfied with their other operations, except that the Federal Reserve Bank of Chicago admitted to complete inability to stimulate business in 1930 through the medium of low rates.

On the question of whether improved methods of handling discount rate changes would render them more effective, some of the Reserve banks showed that they held high hopes of a more potent discount policy in the future. It was the consensus of opinion that larger increases on upward movements would be more effective. Seven of the twelve Reserve banks felt that rate reductions had generally been more effective than rate increases. Only one Reserve bank, Cleveland, thought that the opposite was the case. As to whether rates charged by Reserve banks should be above market rates to render them more effective, there was almost complete unanimity of opinion. Eleven Federal Reserve banks thought that the Reserve bank rates should remain slightly below market rates, as they have been since the close of the war. The Federal Reserve Bank of Chicago hoped for better discount rate control in the future if rates are held above that level.

The ineffectiveness of discount rate policy was generally conceded to be due to the fact that rates charged customers by member banks, especially by those in smaller places, are relatively stable and do not respond to outside stimuli, such as rates ruling at Reserve banks. The question whether rates ruling in the capital markets respond to changes in Reserve bank policy was not considered in the questionnaire but will be examined in this study.

The Reserve banks attempted a further elaboration of discount rate control with a view to controlling the tendency of banks to remain permanently in debt to their Reserve banks or to absorb too large a proportion of their Reserve bank's resources. Such banks were at one time charged a penalty rate. This practice was first permitted by an amendment to the Federal Reserve Act enacted into law on April 13, 1920. The fact that this amendment was passed in 1920 indicates that it was a piece of legislation born in a period of expansion and modeled to deal with particular problems which arose in that period. The permission to charge penalty rates was used but little and, upon complaint of the banks against which it was used, was dropped from practice though not from the statute books in 1921.[8] It was formally repealed by a provision of the Agricultural Credits Act, approved March 4, 1923.

Since 1922 each Reserve bank has had but one rate for all advances to member banks. Before that date each bank had a system of multiple rates varying according to the maturity of the paper offered with preferential rates on trade acceptances, commodity paper and, for the duration of the war, paper secured by government bonds.

Open Market Operations In Bankers' Acceptances

The Reserve banks make certain advances to the money market and, therefore, indirectly to member banks by purchasing bankers' acceptances in the open market at a rate

[8] A description of the quarrel leading to the abandonment of penalty rates may be found in Beckhart, *Discount Policy of the Federal Reserve System*, N. Y., 1924, pp. 405-410.

which is generally lower than the discount rate. This rate is changed more frequently than the discount rate and determines the volume of acceptances bought in the open market. The market rate on acceptances never is more than a small fraction of one percent above the Reserve bank buying rate and is only below that rate at times when the Reserve banks are not an active factor in the bankers' acceptance market. The Reserve banks have, therefore, usually determined the market rate on bankers' acceptances.

Until recently the Reserve banks have claimed that their acceptance buying policy was a part of their discount policy rather than of their open market policy. Their reasoning on this point was on an *a priori* basis and was summarized by the Federal Reserve Board as follows:[4]

> In pursuance of their policy of encouraging the acceptance market, the reserve banks have stood ready at all times to purchase such eligible bills as were offered to them at rates established by the reserve banks. It is because of this policy of the reserve banks to purchase at their buying rates all offerings of eligible bills that reserve bank holdings of bills in their effect upon the credit situation are similar in character to discounts, since they represent for the most part the application of member banks for reserve bank funds. It is, furthermore, the practice of reserve banks never to sell purchased acceptances, but to carry them, like rediscounted paper, to maturity. This is in contrast to purchases and sales of United States securities, which are undertaken at the initiative of the reserve banks in the light of the general credit situation at a rate fixed in the market.

In later years the Reserve banks have abandoned their policy of buying only as many acceptances as were offered to them at previously established buying rates and have, instead, determined the volume which they would purchase,

[4] Federal Reserve Board, *Annual Report*, 1925, p. 8.

fixing their rates accordingly. Whenever the open market rate charged by dealers is altered the Reserve banks alter their buying rates according to whether or not they are buying the quantity of such paper determined upon in advance. In the autumn of 1928 the Reserve banks embarked upon an acceptance buying operation which the Federal Reserve Bank of New York admitted to have had a direct effect upon the money market similar to that exerted by purchases of United States securities.[5] Professor Marcus Nadler, in testifying before the Senate Committee on Banking and Currency in 1931, made the following statement:[6]

> At the present time . . . the reserve banks have used the open market operations as a major instrument of credit control, and the thing which is particularly objectionable is for the reserve banks more or less to tell in advance how many acceptances they will buy in the future.

Further evidence that the Reserve banks have used their acceptance buying policy as a part of their open market policy rather than as a part of their discount policy is shown by the fact that the Open Market Investment Committee has purchased a large part of the acceptances bought for Reserve bank account. The statement of the Reserve Board, quoted above, represents a wish rather than a fact. Furthermore, the usual effect of an increase in open market holdings of acceptances, as well as of government securities, is a reduction of interest rates ruling in the open market, while the effect of an increase in the volume of direct advances to member banks in the form of rediscounts is an increase in open market interest rates. Professor Beckhart has stated in his study of the New York money market that the acceptance buying policy of the Federal Reserve banks should

[5] *Hearings Pursuant to S. Res. 71*, appendix, part 6, p. 796.

[6] *Hearings Pursuant to S. Res. 71*, part 3, p. 505.

be classified with their open market policy.[7] This is the view held by most authorities at present.

The open market operations of the Reserve banks are limited by section 14 of the Act to a few classifications of paper. Some suggestions were made that commercial paper eligible for rediscount be included. For example, Mr. Samuel Untermyer thus criticized the original Glass Bill which preceded the Federal Reserve Act for not allowing purchases of commercial paper: [8]

> Discount rates should be regulated, as they are in other countries, largely by the purchase of bills and acceptances in the open market, whereas this bill provides only for the purchase of bills —that is, domestic bills, through the banks.

Mr. Untermyer feared that the Reserve banks would have no control over the domestic situation without extensive open market powers. But section 14 of the Federal Reserve Act, as originally enacted into law, permitted the Reserve banks to purchase and sell in the open market only " cable transfers and bankers' acceptances and bills of exchange of the kinds and maturities by this Act made eligible for rediscount with or without the endorsement of a member bank." The Board later ruled that the phrase "of the kinds and maturities . . ." limited only the words " bills of exchange " and so permitted bankers' acceptances based on import and export transactions with maturities up to six months to be purchased, though not rediscounted, by Reserve banks.[9] The amendment to the Act of September 7, 1916, added domestic bankers'

[7] B. H. Beckhart, *The New York Money Market*, N. Y., 1932, vol. iii, pp. 448-450.

[8] *Hearings before the Committee on Banking and Currency of the United States Senate, 63rd Congress, 1st Session*, on H. R. 7837 (S. 2639), 1913, pp. 808-1367.

[9] For a discussion of this point see Beckhart, *Discount Policy of the Federal Reserve System*, pp. 169-171, n. 66.

acceptances to the group eligible for rediscount and for open market purchase. But one name commercial paper, the typical American credit instrument, was never admitted to the privilege of purchase by Reserve banks.

Open Market Operations In Government Securities

Purchases of securities of the United States Government as well as of tax anticipation warrants and certain other securities of states, counties and municipalities were permitted under the terms of section 14, paragraph 2 (b) of the Act.

The Reserve banks began early to purchase bankers' acceptances and municipal warrants. During the World War they purchased some short term government securities, although they depended upon Liberty Loan campaigns and bank loans, which might be rediscounted at Reserve banks for investors, to absorb long term government bonds. It was not until 1922 that the purchase of government securities was undertaken on an extended scale. At that time, having a surplus of loanable funds which member banks were unwilling to borrow, the Reserve banks purchased $400,000,000 worth of government securities in the open market.[10] Since an operation of this magnitude would inevitably have a great effect on the money market, particularly in depressing market rates of interest, it was deemed wise to limit the powers of the Reserve banks in such matters in the future. Under the leadership of Governor Strong of the Federal Reserve Bank of New York, a committee was

[10] The reason given later by the Reserve banks was that they needed these securities to enable them to earn their expenses and dividend requirements. The imports of gold which took place in 1921 enabled member banks to pay off their borrowings at Reserve banks and the latter found themselves without earning assets. In this manner the gold imports of 1921 and 1922 were made a part of the credit base and were not "sterilized" as has been claimed.

formed of the governors of the Federal Reserve Banks of Boston, New York, Philadelphia and Chicago to formulate a plan. This committee directed the Reserve banks to sell securities between June, 1922, and July, 1923, principally with a view to assisting the Treasury with its redemption operations but also with a view to restraining the expansion of production and prices which was taking place at that time.[11]

On April 1, 1923, the Board formally constituted this group as the " Open Market Investment Committee " adding to it the governor of the Federal Reserve Bank of Cleveland.

Due to the fact that the committee was absorbing the duties of administering the major credit control policies of the Federal Reserve System and that it was felt that the Board and the interior Reserve banks had too little voice in its actions, the Board discontinued the committee on March 25, 1930. It appointed in its place the Open Market Policy Conference consisting of the governors of the twelve Federal Reserve banks acting under the guidance of the Federal Reserve Board. The Banking Act of 1933 made a Federal Open Market Committee a permanent part of the System by amending the Federal Reserve Act to allow for it. The Committee consists of one member appointed by the board of directors of each Federal Reserve bank and meets four times a year in Washington, D. C., or upon the call of the Governor of the Federal Reserve Board or of three members of the committee. Any member of the Federal Reserve Board may attend the meetings of the committee. In addition to the establishment of a permanent committee, the Banking Act of 1933 forbade independent open market operations by any Reserve bank except in accordance with regulations of the Federal Reserve Board. Thus, the open

[11] This was the reason given by the Reserve banks. See *Hearings Pursuant to S. Res. 71*, part 6, p. 705.

market powers of the Reserve banks have been removed from their individual jurisdictions and placed in the hands of a committee dominated by the Federal Reserve Board.

In answer to the questionnaire referred to above, among the reasons given by the Reserve banks for their frequent open market operations, those which occur most frequently are to make discount rates effective, to influence production, business and commodity prices and to check speculation. In achieving these aims, the Reserve banks did not have great success, according to their own estimates, beyond influencing interest rates. They themselves admitted that they were able, by this method, to influence business conditions or production only twice out of five times they attempted to do so, to influence commodity prices only once out of three attempts and to influence speculation not at all. In their major operation in the spring of 1932 they were able to lower interest rates on government securities almost to the vanishing point and to finance gold exports and currency hoarding without strain on the money market, but not to influence business conditions.

On account of the prominent part in credit policy played by open market operations, much criticism has grown up of their extensive use. Dr. Adolph I. Miller, member of the Federal Reserve Board, has been a critic of the open market policy for several years. As early as April 30, 1928, he made the following statement before the Commitee on Banking and Currency of the House of Representatives: [12]

Let me add, Mr. Congressman, because it is a part of what I was saying, that in my opinion the importance of discount policy as an instrument of credit regulation shall be emphasized by the Federal reserve henceforth and an abridgement of open-

[12] *Hearings before the Committee on Banking and Currency, House of Representatives, 70th Congress, 1st Session, Pursuant to H. R. 11806,* 1928, pp. 125-126.

market operations as a primary instrument of credit policy. I am of the opinion that open-market operations have been the cause of almost as much mischief in credit and economic situations as of good. I am inclined to think that as we get far enough away to review the history of the past four or five years in fuller perspective that conclusion will be justified.

Three years later Dr. Miller stated that there had been too much inflation in the Federal Reserve System and that its favorite instrument of inflation had been the open market purchase of government securities.[13]

In June, 1932, the open market policy of the Federal Reserve System was severely criticised in the report of the Gold Delegation of the League of Nations with Professor Cassel of Sweden dissenting. The report emphasized the fact that the Reserve banks have been using their open market operations to neutralize gold movements while they should have used them to re-enforce the natural effects of gold movements on the money markets both of the country losing gold and of the country receiving it.[14]

Moral Suasion

Besides the discount rate, the buying rate on acceptances and the purchase of securities in the open market the Reserve banks may refuse to rediscount paper offered to them. It has been conceded by the Federal Reserve Board that the discount of paper by a member bank at its Reserve bank is a privilege and not a right. Direct refusal to rediscount was used against banks which were increasing their security loans in 1929. This method of procedure was called "moral suasion" because it was based on the idea that the banks might be persuaded to change their loan policies and that they had a moral responsibility to do so.

[13] *Hearings Pursuant to S. Res. 71*, part 1, p. 147.

[14] League of Nations, Financial Committee, *Report of the Gold Delegation*, 1932.

In answer to the questionnaire referred to above, the Reserve banks, after sober reflection, gave their views as to the efficacy of moral suasion in accomplishing the specific purpose of a reduction in loans to brokers. Eight Reserve banks [15] actually considered it a better method of control than the discount rate for the purpose in hand. They pointed out that outside the metropolitan centers the banks never pass on changes in the discount rate to their customers and, therefore, most customer rates are not influenced by discount rates at all. The Federal Reserve Bank of Atlanta considered the policy good if it were backed up by a high discount rate. The three remaining Reserve banks—Boston, New York and Richmond—preferred rate control. All of the Reserve banks stated that they had used moral suasion at other times in order to control the expansionist tendencies of individual banks whose portfolio policies were considered to be unsatisfactory. In spite of this admission, some of the Reserve banks were less enthusiastic about using the same method of control when most banks have unsatisfactory portfolio policies. During the early part of 1920 some Reserve banks refused to rediscount paper for certain banks which had been using too great a proportion of the resources of their Reserve banks. Much controversy arose at that time as to what proportion of the resources of a Reserve bank a member bank might borrow, and the Reserve banks, unable to cope with this fine question of arithmetic, abandoned their efforts to determine it.[16]

Moral suasion became mandatory by the passage of the Banking Act of 1933. Section 3(a) of this Act requires

[15] Chicago, Cleveland, Dallas, Kansas City, Minneapolis, Philadelphia, St. Louis and San Francisco.

[16] For a more complete account of the use of moral suasion at that time see B. H. Beckhart, *Discount Policy of the Federal Reserve System*, pp. 355-356.

that Federal Reserve banks shall keep themselves informed of the character and amount of the loans of their member banks to ascertain whether " undue use " is being made of bank credit for speculative purposes and that the results of such investigations shall determine whether or not they shall grant accommodation to individual member banks. This provision of the Act represents a radical departure from the policies laid down in the Board's Annual Report for 1928, in which it was stated that banking policy, or supervision over the loan and investment policies of individual banks, has but a limited influence on credit conditions as a whole, for supervision over the loan and investment policies of member banks is now a part of the regular mechanism of credit control. Section 7 of the Act permits the Federal Reserve Board, six members consenting, to fix the percentage of individual bank capital and surplus which may be represented by security loans for each Federal Reserve district. The penalty for non-compliance is again suspension of rediscount privileges. Section 9 of the Act further forbids the increase of loans secured by stocks and bonds or of unsecured loans to stock exchange members or to security dealers by banks which are in debt to their Reserve banks on their own notes secured by deposited collateral.

So far the contról over internal loan and investment policies of member banks has been limited to those member banks which are borrowing or intend to borrow from their Reserve banks. Banks may still expand in any direction which they see fit on the basis of Reserve bank credit extended through open market operations. The Federal Reserve System has never attempted to go further in banking policy than to attempt to hinder speculation. Any attempt to regulate industrial activity through credit control is considered to be contrary to the American way of doing business.

Moral suasion can only influence those banks which are willing to listen to reason. Furthermore, it applies to banks which are in debt to their Reserve banks and to no others. Banks which are increasing their loans on securities frequently do not have to apply for rediscounts as they may be benefiting by clearings and thereby be forcing other banks—ones which are not increasing their security loans—to rediscount. Therefore, moral suasion is of very much more limited use in the United States, where there is a large number of small unit banks, than in Germany—a country where it has been used with greater success because the banks are few in number.

Eligibility and Acceptability Requirements

To influence credit conditions the Reserve banks may use another tool—that is, changing the eligibility and acceptability requirements for notes, drafts and bills of exchange. The Federal Reserve Board exercises the right to decide what kinds of drafts member banks may accept and what kinds of paper Reserve banks may rediscount or purchase in the open market insofar as the provisions of the Federal Reserve Act leave room for interpretation or modification. But the individual Reserve banks have the right to refuse to rediscount paper either because it is not acceptable from a credit standpoint or because the member bank applying for the rediscount is not in a condition to warrant borrowing.

Within the limits set above the Reserve banks may vary their individual requirements to suit the kind of credit control which they wish to exercise. They have done this but little. Only the Federal Reserve Banks of Atlanta and Boston admitted to having tried this method of restricting credit.[17] Otherwise refusal to rediscount had to do with the credit rating of individual notes or of individual member banks rather than with credit conditions in general.

[17] *Hearings Pursuant to S. Res. 71*, appendix, part 6, p. 711.

The Federal Reserve Board may change the type of paper which is acceptable or eligible but its changes, promulgated in rulings which apply to all future paper, are permanent in nature. The contribution of these changes to credit inflation will be discussed in Chapter V and their effects on bank liquidity will be discussed in Chapter IX. Other opinions to the contrary, the Reserve banks did not believe that these changes had had any appreciable effect upon the amount of credit extended throughout the country. Indicating that they did not consider that these rulings had had any inflationary effects, the Reserve banks which wished to have them amended demanded more liberalizations.[18]

Other Methods of Credit Control

Other methods of control are of little importance. Professor Beckhart mentioned two such tools which are permitted under the terms of the Federal Reserve Act. These are (1) the right of the Board to reject the application of any Federal Reserve bank for Federal Reserve notes or else to make an interest charge on that part of the notes granted which is in excess of the amount covered by gold or gold certificates; and (2) to meet emergencies when reserves of Reserve banks are deficient, the right of the Board to suspend temporarily the requirements provided the Reserve

[18] The Chicago Bank suggested extending the maturity date and including paper secured by stocks and bonds in times of emergency. The Dallas Bank suggested including landlords' obligations and extending the fifteen-day member bank collateral note, if the note is collateraled by notes, drafts, bills of exchange or bankers' acceptances, to ninety days at all times. The latter suggestion was adopted in the Banking Act of 1933. The Philadelphia Bank suggested permitting individual banks in distress to rediscount any of their assets. The Richmond Bank suggested the rediscount of notes secured by high grade bonds in emergencies, such paper, however, not serving as security for Federal Reserve notes. *Hearings Pursuant to S. Res. 71*, appendix, part 6, pp. 702, 707-708.

banks pay a graduated tax on the amount of their deficiencies in reserves. The first of these minor tools of control has not been used. The second one possesses the great disadvantage that the public can learn of its previous application through the published weekly statements of condition of the Federal Reserve banks. Nervous fear of the consequences of such knowledge may explain why the expedient was not resorted to at the time when it was most needed—March 4, 1933.

Professor Spahr further mentions the possibility of an agreement between the Federal Reserve Board and the Treasury by which Federal Reserve notes are substituted for gold certificates at times of strain.[19] This substitution appears to have taken place during periods of gold export—1924, 1927 and 1932. It is used to regulate the gold policies of the System rather than its credit policies.

SUMMARY

Of the tools of control possessed by the Federal Reserve System the importance of the discount rate has been greatly overemphasized in the past. The open market tool has grown steadily in importance and is being exercised at the time of writing with a view to influencing directly the volume of member bank credit as well as causing it to expand due to the inducement of low interest rates. Control over open market operations has been gradually centralized, first, by the establishment of committees and conferences and later, under the provisions of the Banking Act of 1933, by the establishment of a permanent Federal Open Market Committee and limitation of the right of any Reserve bank to

[19] W. E. Spahr, *The Federal Reserve System and the Control of Credit*, N. Y., 1931, pp. 49-50. A description of how this expedient was used at different times may be found in S. E. Harris, *Twenty Years of Federal Reserve Policy*, Cambridge, 1933, vol. i, chaps. xix and xx, pp. 341-371.

engage in open market operations on its own initiative. The Reserve banks' right to alter their buying rates on acceptances has been used to influence the acceptance market only but has been admitted to have had more serious effects, particularly in the fall of 1928. Alterations in the eligibility and acceptability requirements for paper purchased or rediscounted by Reserve banks have served to protect the paper, rather than to control the volume of credit in use. The refusal to rediscount, as a device to limit credit expansion qualitatively, has only recently been applied and is now, under the provisions of the Banking Act of 1933, a permanent part of Federal Reserve policy. Other tools of control have been used but little and are, therefore, of little account in explaining past events. The possibility of their use in the future must not, however, be overlooked.

The emphasis placed by all Reserve banks, in their statements published in the Hearings Pursuant to Senate Resolution 71, on their ability to influence market rates of interest indicates that they hold the theory that they have the power to alter the volume of member bank credit through the effect which the rate of interest has upon the desire to borrow. The feasibility of indirect control by means of interest rates must be examined into more closely.

CHAPTER III

History of Federal Reserve Policies

The policies of the Federal Reserve System have been characterized by vacillation and uncertainty of purpose. When account is taken of the additional uncertainty as to the method to be used in attempting to control the money markets, an inevitable confusion in banking practice results.

OBJECTIVES

Before determining upon the aims of Federal Reserve policy, we must define closely the purpose for which the Federal Reserve banks were organized. Their purpose may be to serve as emergency institutions to supply additional reserves to banks at times of crisis, either when all banks are in difficulty or when particular institutions are in sudden need of funds. If the Reserve banks are to serve primarily as emergency institutions, the provision of the excess reserves needed by banks extending credit to agriculture and industry at certain times of year when seasonal strains are felt is not precluded. Thus the seasonal problem is to be dealt with. The purpose of the Reserve banks may be broader, that is, to compete with existing banks by extending credit which banks might otherwise refuse. In choosing among these alternatives the Federal Reserve Board chose a middle course for the guidance of the Reserve banks. In its *First Annual Report* it made the following statement:

The function of a reserve bank is not to be identified with either of these extremes, although occasion may arise when either of such courses may be imperative. Its duty plainly is not to await emergencies but by anticipation, to do what it can to prevent them.

Since the Federal Reserve System has chosen to anticipate emergencies, it must exercise control over the volume of credit extended by commercial banks at all times. It may do this by two means—either through what is called credit policy or through banking policy.

Credit policy implies control over the volume of credit in use. As the credit in use is credit extended by commercial banks, and as the powers of the Reserve banks are limited to the determination of the volume of credit extended by the Reserve banks, effective credit policy presupposes a fixed relationship between commercial bank credit and Reserve bank credit. In determining the volume of Reserve bank credit, the powers of the Reserve banks are also somewhat limited. The volume of Reserve bank credit extended through the mechanism of open market operations is under the direct control of the Reserve banks. But Reserve bank credit extended through the purchase or discount of bills is controlled indirectly by the effect which the rate charged is assumed to have upon the volume brought to the Reserve banks for sale or discount. Effective credit policy is, therefore, dependent upon (1) a unified discount and open market policy and (2) an inverse relationship between the rates charged by the Reserve banks and the volume of Reserve bank credit applied for by member banks, bill brokers, security dealers and others who deal directly with the Reserve banks. Consequently, the financial community may circumvent the policies of the Reserve banks by two means. The first is the extension of varying amounts of commercial bank credit on the basis of a given amount of Reserve bank credit. The second is the demand for increasing amounts of Reserve bank credit at times when Reserve bank rates are high. Credit policy is dictated with a view to guaranteeing that ultimate borrowers' needs for credit recognition are filled.

Banking policy has to do with the supervision of the distribution of the loans and investments of the member banks themselves. Its effectiveness in preventing an overissue of bank liabilities is based on the principle that credit extended for the purpose of moving goods from producer to consumer through the ordinary channels of trade cannot be redundant. Supervision by the Federal Reserve System of a member bank's loan and investment policies could prevent the member bank from borrowing at its Reserve bank to support a portfolio which is being increased with any other end in view. Banking policy is undertaken to protect the bank rather than its borrower.

In spite of the fact that one of the purposes for creating a Federal Reserve Act was to render the banks of the country safe, the Federal Reserve Board has repudiated banking policy as an aim of Federal Reserve policy in favor of credit policy. In its *Annual Report* for 1928 it made the following statement:

> Influence exerted by a reserve bank on the loan and investment policy of an individual member bank is ordinarily exercised only over banks that are borrowers from the reserve banks. It is in the nature of banking supervision, and is akin in many respects to the bank examination function of the reserve system. This phase of reserve bank policy may be called banking policy, as distinguished from credit policy, which deals with more general developments of banking in relation to the credit needs of the country. . . . For influencing general credit conditions, however, the Federal reserve system relies on credit policy rather than on banking policy.

This report goes on to state that the principal aims of credit policy are " the continuous provision of credit at reasonable cost in amounts adequate for the requirements of trade and industry and the safeguarding of our gold reserves."

In exercising the power of altering its discount policy the Federal Reserve System ought to avoid certain pitfalls. The first is the tendency of banks to substitute borrowed reserves for true reserves. Member banks are not permitted to remain continuously in debt to their Reserve banks. Thus, they must have the means of cleaning up their borrowings from time to time. At some times only a few member banks are borrowers. At other times almost all member banks borrow but take turns in paying off their loans, only to renew them in a few days' time. In such cases Reserve bank advances are used to increase the lending powers of member banks—a practice which is contrary to the spirit, if not to the letter, of the law. The System also attempts to avoid the use of its credit facilities to provide reserves behind liabilities extended to speculators.[1]

HISTORICAL SURVEY

The history of the policy of the Federal Reserve System divides itself into six distinct periods in each of which a different policy was pursued. Besides differences in the policy there were differences between the means used to promote the objectives which the System set about to attain.

First Period, Pre-War Policies of the Federal Reserve System, 1914-1916

The first period covers the time from the organization of the Reserve banks until the entry of the United States into the World War. During this time the discount activities of

[1] Federal Reserve Board, *Annual Report*, 1923, p. 33. "The exclusion of the use of Federal reserve credit for speculative and investment purposes and its limitation to agricultural, industrial or commercial purposes thus clearly indicates the nature of the tests which are appropriate as guides in the extension of Federal reserve credit."

the Reserve banks were quiescent. Due to the fact that member banks were required to deposit only a very small part of their reserves in the Reserve banks, they were possessed of ample resources to extend credit without borrowing.[2] Furthermore, the slight deposits of reserves in the Reserve banks during the first two years kept the resources of the Reserve banks small. What there was of them was invested for the most part in open market paper, municipal warrants and a few bankers' acceptances and trade acceptances. The open market purchases were made solely with a view to maintaining earnings in the absence of sufficient demand for rediscounts.

Anticipating the time when there would be more demand for rediscounts, the Board set itself the task of defining paper which should be eligible for rediscount under the provisions of section 13 of the Federal Reserve Act. The Act had merely stated that paper, to be eligible for rediscount, must be " notes, drafts and bills of exchange issued or drawn for agriculture, industrial or commercial purposes or the proceeds of which have been used or are to be used for such

[2] Section 19 of the Federal Reserve Act considerably lowered the reserve requirements of member banks below the amount previously required of national banks. Central Reserve city banks were required to hold as reserves 18 percent of their demand deposits and 5 percent of their time deposits, of which only 7/18 were to be deposited in the Reserve banks. Banks in Reserve cities were required to hold as reserves 15 percent of demand deposits and 5 percent of time deposits. Of these only 3/15 were to be deposited in Rederal Reserve banks during the first twelve months and 1/15 at the end of each six-month period thereafter. Country banks were required to hold 12 percent of demand deposits and 5 percent of time deposits, of which only 2/12 were to be deposited in the Federal Reserve banks during the first twelve months and 1/12 at the end of each six-month period thereafter. The old law required that national banks maintain a reserve of 25 percent for Central Reserve city banks and Reserve city banks and of 15 percent for country banks. Thus deposits freed were 7 percent for Central Reserve city banks, 10 percent for Reserve city banks and 3 percent for country banks as well as a larger percentage of all time deposits.

purposes." Notes, drafts, or bills " covering merely investments or issued or drawn for the purpose of carrying or trading in stocks, bonds, or other investment securities, except bonds and notes of the Government of the United States" were expressly prohibited. In order to define more closely the nature of paper which would be considered eligible for rediscount the Board stated in Old Circular No. 13, issued November 10, 1914, that paper, to be eligible, must be liquid in the orthodox sense of the word. In the words of the circular, bills, to be eligible, " should represent in every case some distinct step or stage in the productive or distributive process—the progression of goods from producer to consumer. The more nearly these steps approach the consumer the smaller will be the amount involved in each transaction as represented by the bill, and the more automatically self-liquidating will be its character." In the light of this definition of liquid paper, the eligibility of each note was judged by the use to which the proceeds of the loan were put, or were to be put, irrespective of whether or not the paper was secured. Trade acceptances, bearing on their face descriptions of the transactions underlying the loans were given preferential treatment by being accorded eligibility for purchase as well as for rediscount and were rediscounted at lower rates than other paper. Commodity paper was also rediscounted at lower rates while discount rates on commercial paper were graduated according to maturity.

In setting their first discount rates, the Reserve banks placed them somewhat above the open market rate on commercial paper though below the rates charged customers for commercial loans at banks. In doing this they hoped to prevent discounting for profit.

Judged from the point of view of its future effects, the most important development of Federal Reserve policy during this period was the amendment to the Federal Reserve

Act enacted into law on September 7, 1916. This amendment substantially altered section 13 of the Federal Reserve Act in two respects. In the first place it created the domestic bankers' acceptance based on goods shipped or stored in warehouses and the bankers' acceptance drawn by bankers in foreign countries for the purpose of furnishing dollar exchange. In the second place member banks were empowered to borrow from Federal Reserve banks for periods of 15 days on their own notes secured by paper eligible for rediscount or by government bonds. This provision made all government bonds held in the portfolios of member banks a part of their potential reserves in addition to loans by the banks collateraled by government bonds. This change was of great significance because member banks were now enabled to obtain reserves at times when there was no demand on the part of their customers for loans which might yield eligible paper.

Second Period, the World War, 1917-1919

The entry of the United States into the World War initiated the second period of Reserve bank activity. The constant issues of certificates of indebtedness and the four issues of Liberty bonds put on the market during the years 1917 and 1918 caused demands on the banks for funds far in excess of their power of expansion based on cash reserves. It became necessary for banks to discount their own notes at their Reserve banks in order to handle their allotments of certificates of indebtedness. Since the need of the government for credit recognition far exceeded the cash savings of the people, the banks were encouraged to lend freely to their customers against the purchase of government bonds and the customers' notes were equally freely rediscounted by the Reserve banks.

Banking resources of the country were further mobilized

by means of the amendment to the Federal Reserve Act enacted into law on June 21, 1917. This amendment lowered the reserve requirements of member banks to 7, 10 and 13 per cent of demand deposits for country banks, Reserve city banks and Central Reserve city banks respectively, which was about the amount which had already been deposited in the Reserve banks up to that date, according to the provisions of the original Federal Reserve Act. Reserve requirements against time deposits were lowered to 3 percent. By this means a certain part of the vault cash of banks and of their deposits in national banks in Reserve cities and in central Reserve cities was freed from being held as reserves and could be used to make loans to purchasers of government bonds.

In order to assist the government to float its issues at low rates of interest the Reserve banks established preferential rates on rediscounts secured by war paper, attempting to make the discount rates on different types of war paper conform to the rates borne by them. Discount rates on commercial paper were sharply graduated according to maturity so that member bank 15-day notes enjoyed a very low rate—that borne by paper of 15-day maturity. At the beginning of the war period some Reserve banks attempted to maintain discount rates on commercial paper above the market rate, though this policy was counteracted by the extensive rediscounts of government bond secured paper at preferential rates. After a while all efforts in the direction of maintaining discount rates above open market interest rates were abandoned.

As the demand for rediscount accommodation rose, the Reserve banks curtailed their purchases of assets in the open market. Some Reserve banks ceased buying municipal warrants at all and the total amount of such paper purchased by the System as a whole shrank to negligible amounts.

All Reserve banks continued to buy some bankers' acceptances in order to promote their purpose of maintaining a market for them. A small part of the government issues of certificates of indebtedness was held temporarily by the Reserve banks. The bulk of Reserve bank earning assets consisted in discounted bills. There was a constant increase in discount of member bank 15-day notes secured by government bonds and in rediscounts of customers' paper so secured. Yet at Reserve banks in agricultural districts, such as Kansas City and San Francisco, rediscounts of commercial and agricultural paper exceeded discounts of notes secured by government bonds during most of the war period. This new demand for agricultural loans resulted from the orders of the government for foodstuffs. The Federal Reserve System tried to discourage the making of loans for non-essential industries.

Immediately upon the close of the war the Reserve banks faced the problem of liquidating the credit based on government securities and of forcing the securities themselves out of the hands of the banks and into the hands of investors. The individual Reserve banks laid plans for accomplishing this end to be carried out by raising the rates of discount on paper secrued by government bonds to levels nearer to those charged for the rediscount of commercial paper. But this program was delayed by the Treasury until after the flotation of the Victory Loan of April and May, 1919. The Victory Loan was only slowly digested and there were issues of certificates of indebtedness by the Treasury throughout the year. The Reserve banks continued to keep rates of discount on paper secured by certificates of indebtedness at the same level as the rates borne by these certificates, instead of forcing the Treasury to pay the rate set by the market. The war-time credit policies of the Federal Reserve System continued throughout most of the year 1919.

In spite of the policy of continuing to accommodate the government, the rediscounts of commercial and agricultural paper were an increasing proportion of Reserve bank advances during the year 1919.

Third Period, the Post-War Liquidation of the Government Debt, 1920–1922

The events of this period, particularly of the years 1920 and 1921, are unique in the history of Federal Reserve policy up to the time of writing. It has only been during this short period of two years that the Reserve banks have ever attempted to perform the function which they were originally intended to perform—financing the short term credit needs of industry. Government bonds were not regarded as an ideal bank asset and investors were encouraged to take them over at whatever price they were willing to pay.

The danger of overexpansion of credit inherent in the mechanism of the Federal Reserve System was recognized and attempts were made to avoid the recurrence of such overexpansion. Governor Harding of the Federal Reserve Board stated in his *Annual Report* for the year 1919:

> The experience of the past three years has demonstrated the expansive power of the Federal Reserve System. It should be understood, however, that an elastic system of reserve credit and note issue implies capacity to control and the ability to curtail credit.

This passage indicates that the Reserve System had abandoned the theory that credit expansion could be automatically checked and the idea of control was thenceforth emphasized.

In its effort to curtail credit the Federal Reserve Board authorized the individual Reserve banks to raise discount rates a number of times beginning in November, 1919. During 1920 the rate on commercial paper and on member bank 15-day notes was raised by steps from 4¾ per cent to

7 per cent at the larger Reserve banks. In the beginning of 1921 this rate stood at 7 per cent at six Reserve banks and at 6 per cent at the remaining ones. Beginning in April, 1921, all Reserve banks commenced lowering rates until they stood between 4½ per cent and 5½ per cent at the close of the year. Rates ruling on paper secured by government obligations were lowered less than were commercial paper rates so that by October fifth there were uniform rates on all types of paper at every Reserve bank. Since that time preferential rates have not been used.

The volume of bills discounted rose and fell with the rates charged on them. This was the cause of comment by some Reserve banks, which had expected the opposite to be the case.[3] The high point for bills discounted for the System as a whole occurred on November 5, 1920, when they totaled 1,827 million dollars, although discounts at some Reserve banks continued to rise during 1921. This indicates the uneven nature of the liquidation. The liquidation took place first in the eastern industrial sections, notably in the Boston district where discounts reached their high point in the end of 1919 and in the New York, Philadelphia, Chicago and St. Louis districts where the liquidation after the peak in the autumn of 1920 was rapid. It came later in the agricultural districts.

The composition of the discount portfolios of the Reserve banks was altered substantially indicating the extent to which the banking system was successful in its effort to drive government bonds out of the banks into the hands of investors. Increases in the volume of bills discounted during 1920 consisted entirely of rediscounts of commercial and agricultural paper. Discounts collateraled by government obligations declined steadily in amount.

[3] See reports of Federal Reserve Agents to the Federal Reserve Board. Report for District No. 7, Chicago, for 1920, Federal Reserve Board, *Annual Report*, 1920, p. 479, is one example.

The Reserve banks were successful in their plan of driving government bonds from bank portfolios, but this action was accomplished at the expense of the holders of these bonds for their price declined rapidly during 1920 and gained but little of the previous loss in 1921. In the year 1921 the Reserve banks noted a great improvement in the investment demand for both long term government bonds and certificates of indebtedness. Some signs of a separate money market in Chicago began to appear. While government securities had previously been dealt in in New York only, the Federal Reserve Agent at Chicago reported in 1921 that there were five recognized local dealers in government bonds who gave daily quotations of prices. Boston also began to develop a separate market both in government securities and in bankers' acceptances, although a majority of the latter were still bought by Reserve banks.

Beginning in May, 1920, gold imports upon an unprecedented scale commenced. By January, 1922, they had amounted to 844 million dollars. The member banks deposited the gold with their Reserve banks as they received it, thus repaying their borrowings. Due to the consequent lack of demand for discounts, the Reserve banks purchased 400 million dollars' worth of government securities during the first five months of 1922. Doing this to enable themselves to earn dividend requirements, they also profoundly influenced money market conditions. This was the first time that the Reserve banks had purchased government securities to any great extent, their open market operations having been almost entirely in bankers' acceptances, trade acceptances and municipal warrants before 1922.

Fourth Period, the Development of Independent Open Market Operations, 1923-1927

This period marked a new attitude toward central banking policy. The difference between this period and previous periods lay in the methods of control used rather than in the aims of control. Where the open market operations of the Federal Reserve System had previously been used to earn expenses and dividends for the Reserve banks, when their resources were not otherwise invested, or to aid in the establishment of regional discount markets, they were now used as a major instrument of credit control. From the time when the Open Market Investment Committee was first formed in 1923, the Reserve banks bought a considerable portion of the United States securities and bankers' acceptances which they held through the committee.

Discount rates during this period came to be of minor importance in the shaping of Federal Reserve policy. Rates were kept consistently below the rates ruling in the open market. Furthermore, the fact that the discount rate was not looked to to act as a means of expressing Federal Reserve policy is attested to by the fact that rates were changed infrequently and some time after open market interest rates —even rates charged by banks in larger cities to their customers—had changed. At the same time the Bank of England was also developing an independent open market policy.[4] Other central banks still depended upon discount rates to exercise control over their banks and money markets.

The major operations in government securities undertaken during this period were the following:[5]

(1) December, 1923, to September, 1924—purchase of $510,000,000.
(2) November, 1924, to March, 1925—sale of $260,000,000.
(3) April, 1926—purchase of $65,000,000.

4 Report of the Committee on Finance and Industry, presented to Parliament, June, 1931, par. 358.

5 *Hearings Pursuant to S. Res. 71*, appendix, part 6, pp. 795-796.

(4) August, 1926, to September, 1926 — sale of $80,000,000.

(5) May, 1927, to November, 1927—purchase of $270,000,000.

Each time that securities were sold, member banks did not restrict their advances to their customers, but increased their rediscounts at Reserve banks. Purchases of securities did not lead to increases in the volume of commercial credit extended, but to increases in the volume of the loans to brokers made by New York City banks.

The effect upon the Reserve banks of their great open market operations in government bonds between 1922 and 1927 was to alter the composition of their portfolios. Government securities became an increasing proportion of the earning assets of the Reserve banks.

Fifth Period, Inflation, 1928-1929

Insofar as concerns the use to which credit built up on the basis of Reserve bank credit was put—the financing of stock speculation—the period under discussion differed from the preceding one only in intensity. This was a period in which the Reserve System attempted to pursue a vigorous deflationary policy with a view to curtailing speculation on the stock exchanges. In fact spokesmen for the System stated on frequent occasions that such was the case, but this policy was counteracted by other forces. The reasons for the failure of the deflationary policy of the Federal Reserve System can be looked for in two places. The first was the large volume of funds available from non-banking lenders for the purpose of making security loans. The second was the unwillingness of the Reserve System itself to concentrate all its efforts upon the accomplishment of its main purpose.

Beginning in January, 1928, the Reserve banks sold their holdings of open market paper in order to curtail credit. By the first week in September their holdings of United States securities had declined by over 400 million dollars and their holdings of bills bought in the open market had been allowed to mature without replacement so that they stood at a figure 200 million dollars below that of the beginning of the year. Discounted bills, however, rose by more than 500 million dollars during the same period. Therefore, the net effect of the open market policy of the Reserve banks during the first eight months of 1928 was to change the composition of the portfolios of the Reserve banks, substituting for government securities and bills bought in the open market discounted bills, most of which were member bank 15-day notes secured by government obligations. This increase in the volume of discounted bills took place in spite of increases in the rates of discount charged by the Reserve banks from 3½ percent in January, 1928, to 5 percent in August of that year.

In September, 1928, the Reserve banks, fearing that legitimate business would lack funds to move crops, did not raise their buying rates on bankers' acceptances as much as open market rates on that type of paper had risen. The result of this rate policy was that the holdings of bills bought in the open market by the Reserve banks increased during the autumn of 1928 by 300 million dollars. Since the volume of bills discounted and of government securities held was the same at the end of the year as at the beginning of September, there was an increase of over 300 million dollars' worth of Reserve bank credit during the course of the year. The net effect of the increase in Reserve bank credit upon member bank credit was to increase member bank loans upon securities.

The situation became worse during 1929. This was in spite of the fact that the Federal Reserve System began the year with a more intensive deflationary policy. When 5 percent discount rates and low holdings of government securities did not prove sufficient to check the use of Federal Reserve funds in the stock market, the Federal Reserve Board resorted to moral suasion to check the growth in discounted bills. On February 7, 1929, the Board wrote to all Federal Reserve banks asking them to refuse discount accomodation to any bank which might be increasing its security loans. There was much complaint from both Reserve banks and member banks against this move but steps were taken by all Reserve banks to put it into effect. At the same time they further disposed of some 50 million dollars' worth of securities and allowed their bill holdings, which had been close to 500 million dollars at the beginning of the year, to run off until they stood below 100 million in the summer. In spite of the moral suasion policy bills discounted increased by about 100 million dallars. During the first week in June the policy was unofficially abandoned.

It is difficult to determine whether or not the policy of moral suasion was successful. Mr. Charles Hamlin, a member of the Federal Reserve Board, claimed that the policy of moral suasion was successful because Reserve bank credit declined between February 9, 1929, and June 8, 1929, while security loans of New York City reporting member banks declined during the same period.[6] But at the same time "all other loans" of reporting member banks increased by a greater amount than they had in any previous four month period. This extraordinary increase leads us to believe that there was some shift of security loans to the unsecured category by banks which wished to accommodate those of their customers who were in need of funds to carry securities, at the same time concealing the fact from their Federal Reserve banks.

[6] *Hearings Pursuant to S. Res. 71*, part 1, pp. 167-169.

On August 9, 1929, the Board once again changed its tactics and permitted the Federal Reserve Bank of New York to raise its discount rate to 6 percent, which the Bank had been attempting to do continuously since February 14th. At the same time, the New York Reserve Bank lowered its buying rate on acceptances of all maturities from 5¼ percent to 5⅛ percent. The result of this double move was an increase in bills bought in the open market by all Reserve banks of close to 300 million dollars up to the end of October and a consequent increase in loans on securities of reporting member banks. With the continuing increase in loans to brokers by others than banks, the stock exchange was as active as before, although business had already begun to decline. At the end of October the stock market boom fell under the weight of its own excesses. This leads us to the next period of Federal Reserve policy.

Sixth Period, the Depression of 1929-1933

In attacking the problen of this depression the Federal Reserve System commenced by dealing only with a stock market crisis, on the assumption that the latter was an isolated phenomenon. In handling the stock market crisis, the System made the further assumption that it was a temporary affair which would be cured when prices on the stock exchange had risen to a point between the high level of September, 1929, and the level of December. Proceeding on these assumptions the Reserve banks increased their holdings of government securities by 350 million dollars between the panic and the end of the year. This move enabled banks to take over a part of the one and one half billion dollars' worth of loans to brokers which had been made by " others " who wished to withdraw their funds. Thus, the System departed for the time being from the rule that it was not ready to assist the banks in lending to speculators.

After the stock exchange panic had been folowed by a depression the Reserve banks tried to deal with the general industrial stagnation by lowering interest rates by any means whatsoever. They tried both extensive security purchases and lower discount rates. By September 16, 1931, United States securities held by the System increased by 230 million dollars beyond the amount held at the end of 1929, in spite of the fact that the cash reserves of the System had increased due to gold imports by almost 650 million dollars during the same period. The Federal Reserve Bank of New York also lowered its discount rate a number of times until it reached 1½ percent on May 8, 1931. The rates ruling at the other Reserve banks were as low as 2, 2½, and 3 percent in the summer of 1931. In spite of these low rates, the volume of bills discounted at Reserve banks shrank steadily. At the height of the speculative era they had stood at 1,081 million dollars in spite of the 5 and 6 percent rates then ruling. On September 16, 1931, when rates at Reserve banks were at their lowest, the volume of bills discounted was only 263 million dollars and it had been lower during the summer.

On September 21, 1931, an event occurred which completely altered the policies of the Reserve banks for a short period of time. The abandonment of the gold standard by Great Britain caused a drain on the gold reserves of the Federal Reserve System. The alarm felt by foreign banks, particularly the Bank of France, that America might follow the example of Great Britain led these institutions to withdraw their New York balances. The Reserve banks made no effort to counteract the effects of the gold movement by security purchases but they were forced to take over the bankers' acceptance market, the volume of bills held by them standing at a point 700 million dollars above the lowest point for the year in the middle of October. At the same time the volume of bills discounted rose to over one billion dollars by the end of the year and discount rates at all Reserve banks were raised, the rate at New York being 2 percent above its low point. This reversal of the depression policy of the Federal Reserve System was said to have been made at the behest of the Bank of France.

When the storm was over in 1932, the Reserve banks once again attempted to stimulate credit expansion through the establishment of low money rates. The fact that the Treasury had been forced to increase its indebtedness ever since the close of the fiscal year 1930 may have been one factor inducing the Reserve banks to purchase one billion dollars' worth of government securities in the spring of 1932. But the fiction that this measure was started to aid the money market was maintained by having the Reserve banks buy from the market, as they always had done, instead of from the Treasury directly as they might as well have done, since new government issues amounted to more than one billion dollars during that period. The actual effects of this purchase were the piling up of reserves in excess of those required by law by member banks and an increase in the balances held by them for the account of other banks. The bankers' balances held by member banks increased 626 million dollars during 1932, while the excess reserves of these banks increased 466 million dollars.[7] Consequently larger member banks were in a position of great vulnerability in case of any mass demands for currency on the part of smaller banks. Thus, the open market purchase of securities by the Reserve banks in 1932 was one factor leading up to the crisis and closing of all banks in 1933.

[7] The increase in New York City and Chicago alone was 421 million dollars. These excess reserves were concentrated in larger places and represented the excess reserves of smaller banks. Due to the prevailing habit of hoarding they should have been held in the form of cash and reserve balances, but only two thirds of them were so held.

In the meantime the Reserve banks had again lowered their discount rates—the rate ruling at the New York Bank having been lowered to 2½ percent during the first six months of 1932. These low rates, as was the case with previous low rates, did not serve as incentives to borrowing, either by member banks from their Reserve banks or by customers of member banks from them.

Changes in the rediscount provisions of the Federal Reserve Act have been instituted during 1932 and 1933, which, if made permanent, will completely eliminate the commercial character of that part of Reserve bank assets which has withstood the pressure of the changes of the decade 1922 through 1932.

Due to the complaint that many banks no longer had eligible assets, the Glass-Steagall Act of February 27, 1932, provided (1) for the discount of the notes of groups of five or more member banks which have no eligible assets with the consent of at least five members of the Federal Reserve Board; and (2) for the discount for any member bank with a capital of less than $5,000,000, in "exceptional and exigent circumstances," of ineligible assets, provided the assets pledged are satisfactory to the Federal Reserve bank and the consent of at least five members of the Federal Reserve Board be obtained. Since few Federal Reserve funds were put into circulation by this means, the Emergency Relief and Construction Act of July 21, 1932, permitted the rediscount by Reserve banks of notes, drafts and bills of exchange of the kinds and maturities made eligible for discount for member banks for individuals, partnerships or corporations with the consent of at least five members of the Federal Board, provided such individuals, partnerships or corporations have no other sources of funds. Both of these acts were made temporary but subject to renewal. The Glass-Stegall Act, whose one year lease on life has twice expired, has both times been renewed.

The Emergency Bank Act of March 9, 1933, further broadened the discount powers of the Federal Reserve banks. Under exceptional and exigent circumstances Federal Reserve banks are empowered by this Act to make advances to member banks which have no eligible assets on their own promissory notes " secured to the satisfaction of such Federal reserve bank." This provision is also of one year's duration, but may be extended for such periods as the President of the United States shall prescribe.

At the same time the Banking Act of 1933 was enacted into law, and made many restrictions upon rediscounting by member banks which were making security loans. The apparent contradiction between the provisions of the Banking Act of 1933 and the Emergency Bank Act of 1933 can only be explained by the history of these acts. The former was the result of long study undertaken by conservative members of Congress, begun some years before. The latter was the result of presidential orders received by Congress during the time when banks were closed in March, 1933.

The effects of the legislation of 1932 and 1933 cannot be judged at the time of writing. If the provisions of the emergency acts enumerated above are availed of to any great extend the Acts will have to be renewed upon frequent occasions. The protection afforded to bank reserves by the liquidity of the Federal Reserve banks will be lost. There will be substituted for this protection a new type of assurance of repayment—the assurance based upon the power to issue currency without limit, provided by the suspension of the gold standard by the United States.

AN EVALUATION OF FEDERAL RESERVE POLICIES

The discount policy of the Federal Reserve System has been ineffective in bringing about changes in the volume of bills discounted as long as the System has been in operation.

Each time when rates were high the volume of bills discounted rose and low rates were coincident with few bills discounted.

The fault in discount policy, making the rates ineffective to stimulate or to check borrowing, may have been fundamental or it may have been one of method. If the fault is one of method, it might be remedied by maintaining rates of discount above market rates of interest on loans of the type expanded on the basis of discount accommodation, by changing rates more promptly or by unifying the discount and open market policies of the System.

The Federal Reserve banks have made no attempt to maintain their rates above market rates of interest except in the first two years of their operation. Even at that time they held their rates below those charged to the best customers by banks in larger centers. After the close of the war their rates were constantly below rates ruling on prime commercial paper in the open market. The Reserve banks made some efforts to justify this position by pointing out that their rates were consistently above the rates on prime bankers' acceptances. The Federal Reserve Agents and the Federal Reserve Board reminded the public on frequent occasions that rediscounted paper was more like a bankers' acceptance than like open market commercial paper because it had a bank endorsement as well as commercial endorsements. This argument is rationalization rather than fact for two reasons. First, the Reserve banks do not fix their rates with a view to charging for the risk involved, but with a view to accommodating commerce and business. Second, the Reserve banks do not in practice rediscount bankers' acceptances, although they are permitted to do so, because they purchase banker's acceptances in the open market at lower rates.

Any effort to maintain discount rates above market rates of interest presupposes the existence of a money market in each Federal Reserve district. Very few centers have what could be called money markets. But if the element of competition is present in the granting of loans by banks to their customers, there is a market in bank loans. In 1931, the Federal Reserve banks reported their opinions on the question of whether money markets existed in their districts to the Senate Committee on Banking and Currency.[8] Reserve banks outside the great financial centers—New York, Boston, Chicago and San Francisco—thought that customer rates on mortgages could be taken as indicative of market rates in their districts. Some held that rates ruling in the New York market should be followed because funds of banks in outside districts are invested in the New York market, which amounts to an admission that there is no market rate in the districts in question. Some Reserve banks made the suggestion that rates charged by banks to customers who can obtain accommodation in more than one district or at more than one bank to be taken as indicative of market rates of interest. Reserve banks in districts where bankers' acceptances are available, with the exception of the Federal Reserve Bank of Chicago, thought that the bankers' acceptance rate should be included in any computation of open market interest rates although the Reserve banks themselves had always up to that time constituted the market for such paper. Thus, the Reserve banks themselves showed very little comprehension of the nature of a money market. While there was disagreement as to whether Reserve bank discount rates influenced customer rates in financial centers, all Reserve banks agreed that discount rate changes are not passed on to customers of country banks.

[8] *Hearings Pursuant to S. Res. 71*, appendix, part 6, pp. 748-793.

In spite of the opinion of most Reserve banks that there were some rates ruling in their districts which could be considered to be measures of market rates, only three Reserve banks—Chicago, Cleveland and St. Louis—thought that discount rates should be held above market rates. While eight Reserve banks were against the practice, the Federal Reserve Bank of New York held that if rates were raised to that level, it would be necessary for the Reserve banks to "release" more credit through open market operations so that member banks would seldom have to borrow. This proposal condones the practice of banks to entend credit on the basis of borrowed reserves—a practice contrary to the previously stated objectives of the Federal Reserve System.

Even though discount rates were held above customer rates at banks, they would be ineffective in preventing discounting for profit, unless they were always above rates ruling in markets where banks invest their secondary reserves. It is not difficult to hold discount rates above the yields of government securities. But a large part of the secondary reserves of banks are loaned on call in the New York market and the call loan rate is subject to such violent fluctuations that discount rates would have to show more extreme cyclical swings in order to be at all times above call loan rates. Since discount rates have never been held at that point, except at times when call loan rates were low and very little discounting was taking place, it is impossible to judge from past experience whether the volume of bills discounted would be contracted when rates are raised under this plan. The experiment might be worth trying.

The greatest obstacle to effective discount policy has been the excessive use of open market operations as separate instruments of credit control. Increases in Reserve bank credit extended through purchases of securities in the open market have resulted in extensions of commercial bank credit based on security transactions. This credit resists liquidation and, therefore, the banks prefer to rediscount rather than to call loans at times of sale of their open market holdings by the Reserve banks. For this reason the open market sale of securities does not serve as an instrument of credit contraction.

SUMMARY

Reviewing the experience of the past twenty years, the policies of the Federal Reserve System have been rendered ineffective by a growing dependence upon the government debt as a source of Reserve bank credit. This trend arose at the time of the World War, although it was brought to an abrupt halt by subsequent efforts to make investors take over the debt. But four years after the cessation of hostilities the government debt once again became the principal Reserve bank asset. A close relationship between the Reserve banks and the Treasury results in an equally close relationship between member banks and the speculative markets, for member bank credit may be extended on the basis of assets which do not yield eligible paper. Consequently it is the duty of the Reserve banks to extend no credit to groups which they cannot control by buying large blocks of securities in the open market and to supervise the internal loan policies of their member banks.

CHAPTER IV

Federal Reserve Policy And The Commercial Credit System

FUNDAMENTAL DEFINITIONS

Credit

Credit has already been defined as an asset of all members of the community taking the form of potential rights over future goods and services which they may exchange for present goods and services. Credit rests, in the last analysis, on future market values of goods.[1] Therefore, the volume of credit is related closely to the production of goods and the price level. When credit is recognized by a seller it results in the creation of purchasing power and is referred to as credit which has been extended.

Categories of Credit

Credit may be divided into categories according to the length of the period of time before the rights to future values mature and become present values. This division is not definite, but two main categories emerge according to the type of present values which are obtained in return for the credit extended. The first refers to what are called current transactions and is known as commercial credit. Commercial credit is credit exchanged for goods which are used only once by the borrower, their disposal bringing about an extinction of the entire amount of credit extended. Investment credit, on the other hand, is credit exchanged for

[1] The word, goods, will be used hereafter to mean both physical goods and services which possess enchange value.

goods which may be used repeatedly to produce other goods which, when sold, give the borrower the disposal of purchasing power sufficient to extinguish only a part of the credit originally extended, until repeated production of new goods have taken place. Such goods are called capital goods and include land, buildings and machinery.

Both commercial and investment credit are further divisible into an infinite number of categories according to maturity. But this division is of no account provided the maturity of the loan corresponds to the length of the economic process underlying the need for the loan.

Further classifications of credit may be made according to the industry using its credit, the type of borrower—whether an individual, a privately owned corporation or a public body, etc.—or according to whether the credit is productive or consumptive. Consumption credit is less well protected than credit which enters into the productive process and, therefore, carries a higher rate of interest. It is usually granted by specialized corporations except in the case of mortgages on land and buildings. But when it is recognized it is the basis for additional issues of purchasing power and, therefore, is of economic importance. Furthermore, much credit whose form makes it appear to be productive credit, is actually consumption credit—for example bank loans to business men who actually use the proceeds to purchase consumers' goods for themselves and their families.

Credit Analysis

The function of credit analysis is to determine the soundness of a loan—i. e., its risk—and whether it is commercial—i. e, is related to the economic process of production and trade. For this purpose three distinct methods of credit investigation or a combination of all three may be used.

The first method of credit investigation is an attempt to relate the extension of credit to the transaction for which the purchasing power created is to be used. In doing this the credit rating must be related to the contemplated future transaction rather than to the past transaction; for if bank advances are related to past transactions only the volume of credit extended by banks will be static—there will be no possibility of expansion for new enterprises. This method of credit analysis takes no account of transactions of the borrower other than the one on which the credit rests.

The second method of credit investigation depends upon an investigation of the general standing of the firm offering its credit, particularly of its possession of working capital. A firm having ample working capital gives evidence that it is in a position to engage in commercial transactions if purchasing power is made available to it. Therefore, the creation of purchasing power on the basis of the working capital of business firms is consonant with the self-liquidating theory of commercial credit, which relates the volume of purchasing power outstanding to the volume of goods going to market. This way of investigating credit is applied by means of appraisals and of analyses of financial statements.

The third method of credit investigation depends upon the deposit of collateral. Since the deposit of collateral assures payment only in case the collateral can be marketed at or near its loan value, the soundness of a collateral loan depends upon the type of collateral deposited. Collateral representing rights to goods in the process of production or marketing is less likely to depreciate than is collateral representing rights to capital goods, whose market values depend upon the market values of their products and the rate of interest at which these values are capitalized. For this reason collateral loans secured by goods destined for ultimate consumption are more sound that are collateral loans secured by stocks and bonds. But the deposit of collateral, while decreasing the risk of non-payment of a loan, does not constitute evidence that the loan is for a commercial purpose, especially where the collateral is non-perishable and, therefore, a type of goods which may be used for speculation. Hence, collateral loans cannot be said to be liquid, unless there be other proof to this effect.

COMMERCIAL CREDIT INSTRUMENTS

There are but two types of commercial credit instruments. These are notes and bills. A note is drawn by a borrower and a bill by a lender. In the latter case the bill is not an evidence of indebtedness unless the borrower acknowledges the debt by acceptance.

Notes may be single name notes or endorsed notes. The frequency with which endorsements are traded or given as accommodation renders them of little value so that the one name note is the commonest form of instrument representing good borrowing in the United States.

Notes may further be differentiated according to the area within which they circulate. They may represent loans made by banks to depositors in which case they remain in the banks. Or note brokers may lend on one name notes, then marketing the notes to small or distant banks—a common method of credit extension in the United States and one which has the double advantage of enabling borrowers, who want larger sums than the legal limitations on bank loans to one interest enable their depository banks to provide, to receive accommodation and also of enabling banks in small places to diversify their portfolios both industrially and geographically.

One name notes are seldom given in return for goods purchased but are more frequently used by sellers of goods who borrow at their banks in order to replenish stocks pending payment of open account loans to their customers. In some cases customers' notes are discounted by banks, the sellers' names appearing on the notes as endorsements. But the discount of open accounts receivable is a risky business, engaged in for the most part by specialized corporations which are not banks of deposit, although accounts receivable are taken into consideration in estimating the working capital of sellers who borrow at banks.

Bills take the form of trade acceptances or bank acceptances. The latter serve limited purposes and will be treated in a separate chapter. Trade acceptances are used only in cases where the borrower is little known or has the reputation of paying slowly. For this reason they are found in trades where credit terms are long such as the jewelry trade and the leaf tobacco industry. They may be discounted by banks but generally represent poorer risks than notes, behind which are the accounts of the better customers.

THE FEDERAL RESERVE SYSTEM AND COMMERCIAL CREDIT INSTRUMENTS

Since one purpose of the Federal Reserve System was to improve, standardize and render more liquid commercial credit instruments, the history of the markets for these instruments under the Federal Reserve System throws light on the extent of the success or failure of these objectives.

Commercial Loans of Banks

The commercial loans of banks have been declining in importance since 1925. It would appear that the tendencies going on during the past nine years have resulted in a declining importance of commercial credit. Whether the Federal Reserve System has been responsible for the decline in the commercial loan is a question which cannot be answered until a complete survey of other forms of credit has been made. If Federal Reserve policy has been a factor causing an overstimulation of competing forms of borrowing, the System may be said to have had an indirect responsibility in causing the decline in commercial paper.

The commercial loans of national banks, as evidenced by a rough measure consisting of all loans not secured by stocks and bonds or by real estate, have not varied in amount with the volume of Reserve bank credit. The Federal Reserve System may have an influence upon the volume and type of commercial credit if the desire of banks to hold eligible paper is so great that they attempt to reduce the amount of ineligible loans which they make. Because government securities held by member banks may be used for borrowing from Reserve banks, the inducement to make loans in such a form that they will be eligible has not been effective. A steady decline in the amount of eligible paper held by national banks in spite of changing economic conditions is shown by the following table:

TABLE 1

Date End of June	*Eligible Commercial Paper Held by National Banks*	*Total Loans of National Banks*	*Commercial Loans of National Banks* *	*Proportion of Total Loans which is Eligible*	*Proportion of Commercial Loans which is Eligible*
	(Millions of dollars)			(percent)	
1923	3,564	11,818	8,372	30.3	42.6
1924	3,542	11,979	8,338	29.6	42.5
1925	3,413	12,674	8,376	26.9	40.8
1926	3,497	13,418	8,655	26.0	40.4
1927	3,362	13,956	8,455	24.1	39.8
1928	3,267	15,145	8,745	21.6	37.4
1929	2,974	14,801	8,092 †	20.1	36.8
1930	2,719	14,888	7,789 †	18.3	34.9
1931	2,159	13,177	6,929 †	16.4	31.2
1932	1,650	10,282	5,285 †	16.0	31.2

Compiled from U. S. Comptroller of the Currency, *Annual Reports*.

* Estimated from loans not secured by stocks, bonds or real estate.

† Basis of reports changed.

Thus it can be seen that one purpose of the Federal Reserve System, that of setting up standards of good commercial paper with a view to inducing the banks to lend according to those standards, has failed of realization.

The Open Market for Commercial Paper

This market is a small one. The industries having recourse to it are limited in number and it is a source of credit supplementary to others. The credit standing of the borrowers must be high and this fact eliminates many small businesses. The amount of commercial paper outstanding with a maturity of less than seven months as reported by the principal dealers to the Federal Reserve Bank of New York reached its post-war high point in January, 1920, when it was $1,296,000,000. In June, 1920, loans of all banks in the United States were $30,650,000,000. Since that time commercial paper has declined both relatively and absolutely in amount. On June 30, 1932, commercial paper reported to the same source was $103,000,000 while total loans of all banks stood at $27,834,000,000. In spite of its small size the market is important because much of this type of paper is eligible for rediscount at the Reserve banks under the same conditions as the notes given by better customers in return for loans at their own banks. Furthermore, it has been subject to very little artificial control and so the commercial paper rate is followed by many as indicative of the level which market rates of interest would reach if forces of demand and supply were allowed to act unhampered.[2] Yet this market is a small part of the custo-

[2] Indicating the importance attached to the commercial paper rate, Mr. Wiggin of the Chase National Bank stated before a subcommittee of the Committee on Banking and Currency of the United States Senate, "I should like to see the Federal reserve rate higher than the market rate and, by the market rate I do not mean necessarily the extreme rates on call money, but what we do consider the market rate for the best commercial paper." *Hearings Pursuant to S. Res. 71*, part 1, p. 184.

mers' loan market which also produces paper eligible for rediscount. In the middle of 1932, when the volume of commercial paper outstanding was $103,000,000, member banks reported $2,428,000,000 of eligible paper in their possession, exclusive of government bonds.

In studying fluctuations in the amount of commercial paper outstanding, we must consider the source of the paper and the principal demand for it. Foulke, on the basis of data collected in 1925, has concluded that the middle-sized corporation is the largest borrower in this market.[3] 55.5 percent of the paper reported on that date originated from corporations with a net worth between $500,000 and $2,500,000. Larger corporations borrow by means of security flotations; while smaller ones, having poorer credit, must borrow directly at their banks. Middle sized corporations may have recourse to the securities markets if times are propitious. Therefore, shifts in the ability of middle-sized corporations to borrow in the securities markets will cause fluctuations in the amount of commercial paper outstanding. The borrowers were principally in the food and textile industries. Therefore, factors affecting the dollar volume of operations in these industries also affect the volume of commercial paper outstanding.

On the demand side, we find that the bulk of the paper offered finds its way into the portolios of banks. The proportion bought by country banks to that bought by banks in larger places varies. Banks in larger places buy more at times when rates are low and country banks buy more when rates are high. Between October 3, 1928, a time of comparatively low interest rates, and October 4, 1929, when rates were high, the Reserve city member banks decreased their holdings of commercial paper from 57.3 percent to

[3] Foulke, *The Commercial Paper Market*, N. Y., 1931, p. 51.

46.8 percent of the total held by member banks. During the subsequent period of decline in interest rates they increased their holdings while country banks decreased theirs, so that on June 30, 1931, they held 73.7 percent of the total. Late in 1931, interest rates rose. The reduction in holdings by Reserve city member banks at that time was more than that by country member banks so that they held 66.2 percent of the total on December 31 of that year. Thus, it will be seen that the rate of interest affects the demand for commercial paper from country banks. The refusal of country banks to buy when rates are low is somewhat balanced by the willingness of banks in larger places to take up the slack when there is one.

The willingness of banks to lend has less to do with the amount of open market commercial paper outstanding than has the desire of business firms to borrow. For this reason we must look for causes of the fluctuations in the amount of commercial paper in the ability of corporations to float other securities at a reasonable rate of interest and the relative prosperity or depression of the industries which borrow in this market, rather than in Federal Reserve policy. The rate of interest, while it has little effect upon the demands of banks for this type of investment, has a great influence upon the exercise of the borrower's choice in determining whether to use this or other markets.[4]

The rate of interest on commercial paper is sensitive to rate changes in other parts of the money market. As the relative position of rates on commercial paper and yields on long term securities have an influence on the volume of commercial paper outstanding, the Federal Reserve System may encourage or discourage the use of this market by means of its influence over the rate of interest. This sub-

[4] Charts 18 and 22 in Chapter VIII show a comparison between the commercial paper rate and the volume of commercial paper outstanding.

ject will be treated in more detail in Chapter VII of this study.

Open market commercial paper has been a very sound type of investment for banks. Foulke has shown that the losses incurred by banks on commercial paper have been almost insignificant as compared to losses on other parts of their portfolios. Further evidence of the soundness of commercial paper is indicated by the rapidity with which this type of credit was extinguished in 1920 and 1921, reaching a low point before other kinds of credit and again by the rapidity of the decline in 1931 and 1932. This does not prove that there was not a shift into other forms of loans which are themselves less sound. It would be impossible to prove that this was the case because data are not available. But it is evident that borrowers must use the proceeds of loans at their own depository banks to take up commercial paper as it matures if they cannot meet it out of receipts obtained in the ordinary course of business.[5]

The Federal Reserve System has given no encouragement to the open market for commercial paper and its methods. Reserve banks stand willing to rediscount notes for banks provided the notes conform to their regulations as to maturity and eligibility as judged by the use to which the proceeds of the loans are to be applied. They will not purchase these notes in the open market for the Federal Reserve Board has ruled that only two name paper in the form of the acceptance is eligible for purchase under the terms of section 14 of the Federal Reserve Act. In its rulings the Board has consistently required that greater emphasis be placed upon the self-liquidating nature of the transaction underlying the loan than upon the credit stand-

[5] Foulke considers the policy of borrowing "from depository banks for from four to six months, then on the open market, back to the banks, and then on the open market again" to be a sound one. *Op. cit.*, p. 55.

ing of the borrower. For this reason it has given greater encouragement to a credit instrument which was in use in only a limited field before the passage of the Act, the trade acceptance.

The Trade Acceptance

At the time of the passage of the Federal Reserve Act the Board saw the possibility of furtherance of the use of this credit instrument by inducing better buyers to accept drafts rather than to buy on open account. It was hoped that the trade acceptance would eliminate abuses growing out of open account charging, such as allowing bills to run past due or borrowing for other than commercial purposes. In the hearings before the Banking and Currency Committee of the United States Senate on the so-called Glass Bill, which preceded the enactment of the Federal Reserve Act, Mr. Samuel Untermyer stated, " That form of obligation (promissory note) is likely to cover up and confuse the difference between commercial transactions and other transactions . . . with the use of an acceptance the paper better explains itself." [6]

Some proponents of the trade acceptance system have hoped that it would eventually result in the abandonment of cash discounts allowed to purchasers for prompt payment. Cash discounts have led to abuses, such as the taking of the discount after the discount period has elapsed. If these discounts were abandoned there would be a shift of much commercial borrowing from the banks of buyers of goods to those of sellers. Before the passage of the Federal Reserve Act, members of the Senate Committee on Banking and Currency raised the question as to whether there would not result

[6] *Hearings before the Committee on Banking and Currency, United States Senate, 63rd Congress, 1st Session,* 1913, *Pursuant to H. R. 7837 (S. 2639)*, vol. i, p. 846.

a shift of financing from banks in smaller places to banks in larger places, due to the concentration of wholesale business and manufacturing in the larger centers. No such shift has actually taken place since the trade acceptance has not displaced the cash discount. The cash discount appears to be firmly rooted in American business practice. It has been estimated that about 50 per cent of buyers take cash discounts. Therefore, the trade acceptance is likely to be used for 50 percent of the accounts only and those would be the poorer ones. One name paper of buyers should, therefore, have a higher credit rating in the market.

The Federal Reserve banks have given artificial stimulus to the trade acceptance market. Until graduated discount rates were done away with in 1920 and 1921 the Reserve banks rediscounted trade acceptances at a preferential rate, usually one eighth of one percent below the rediscount rate on commercial paper. Trade acceptances have been accorded eligibility for purchase in the open market by Reserve banks, a privilege not accorded to commercial paper.

The history of the trade acceptance under the Federal Reserve System has been an illustration of the stability of custom and usage and of their persistance in the face of propaganda. Buying on open account and credit extension by means of one name promissory notes has continued to be the rule for the better accounts. Trade acceptances have been used for the most part for slow or doubtful accounts or as collection instruments for past due bills.

Some trade acceptances are of sufficient merit to be eligible for rediscount or purchase at the Reserve Banks. But the bulk of paper offered for rediscount is paper of other forms, chiefly promissory notes based on commercial or agricultural transactions. This makes discussions of the advantages and disadvantages of the trade acceptance seem highly theoretical. What is the advantage of a credit instrument which virtually does not exist?

The following table shows the volume of trade acceptances and of other commercial paper purchased or rediscounted by the Reserve banks. Rediscounts collateraled by United States government obligations as well as rediscounts of bankers' acceptances are omitted.

TABLE 2

TRADE ACCEPTANCES IN RESERVE BANK PORTFOLIOS

Year	*Volume of Bills Discounted* — *Based on Trade Acceptances*	*Volume of Bills Discounted* — *Based on Other Commercial and Agricultural Paper* *	*Percent of Commercial Paper Discounted Represented by Trade Acceptances*	*Volume of Trade Acceptances Bought in the Open Market*
	(thousands of dollars)			
1915	1,959	159,394	1.2	31
1916	5,212	202,659	2.5	16,333
1917	37,771	3,047,059	1.2	30,948
1918	187,373	6,175,481	2.9	61,036
1919	138,420	4,848,270	2.8	36,558
1920	192,157	27,688,699	0.7	74,627
1921	128,944	25,704,727	0.5	7,166
1922	44,272	6,573,973	0.7	6,309
1923	51,393	8,550,519	0.6	13,540
1924	38,325	3,613,608	1.0	8,452
1925	23,688	7,827,724	0.3	4,765
1926	20,316	9,469,972	0.2	5,591
1927	15,897	7,763,790	0.2	4,811

Compiled from Federal Reserve Board, *Annual Reports*. Data on volume of transactions not available after 1927.

* All bills discounted except those secured by government obligations and trade acceptances.

Since the bulk of these drafts are held by the drawer until maturity and not discounted at any bank, it is impossible to make any estimates of the amount of such credit outstanding at any time. The closest estimate obtainable is in a report of the Trade Acceptance Committee of the American Bankers' Association made in 1921 which stated, "In 1916 the known users of trade acceptances numbered 185. In October, 1920, the list exceeded 20,000. The number has grown steadily since."[7] No authority is given for this statement and it is difficult to determine whether it was the result of an investigation or of a sanguine guess. Lacking better statistics, the volume of trade acceptances rediscounted by the Reserve banks or bought by them in the open market will have to be used as an indication of the increase or decrease in the use of this instrument for the better class of current transactions.

The heyday of the trade acceptance, if such it may be called, was the time from 1918 through 1920. In October, 1917, the American Trade Acceptance Council was formed from a group composed of the Chamber of Commerce of the United States, the American Bankers' Association and the National Association of Credit Men. This organization, with the help of press and pamphlets, launched a campaign to induce business men to change their habits of buying and selling. For the duration of the war patriotic motives led to a slight furtherance of this credit instrument, as shown by Table 2. At the close of the war the tendency to return to old methods began to appear. In January, 1919, recognizing that there was but little business to be had, the Council was reorganized and changed its name to the American Acceptance Council, broadening its activities to include the bankers' acceptance, which had begun to appear in fairly large volume in the American money market. But the campaign for the trade acceptance, so valiantly begun, was not to be abandoned for several years. Trade Acceptance Committees were formed by the American Banker's Association, the American Acceptance Council and other organizations and their resolutions were featured in the *Acceptance Bulletin,* the official organ of the Council.

[7] *Acceptance Bulletin*, Oct., 1921, p. 4.

When the depression of 1920 and 1921 arrived, it brought with it a tying up of credit in all lines. It was quickly observed even by friends of the trade acceptance that misuses in practice had crept in. The ones deserving mention are (1) the renewal of maturing drafts by new ones, (2) the use of the trade acceptance as a collection instrument for unpaid accounts and (3) the omission of the credit investigation which should accompany every lending transaction. Further complaints were made against the banks which appeared to have learned but little about the handling of this instrument. As late as 1923, it was found that banks receiving such paper would often send it to some correspondent bank other than the one at which payment was to be made and that this bank would then request the acceptor to come to its own office on the due date and pay the debt, a method of settlement which is inconvenient. The *Acceptance Bulletin* repeatedly published statements to the effect that a trade acceptance had the bank of payment specifically named on its face and should be cleared just as a check is cleared. It was in fact the same thing as a check, when the due date had arrived. The collection of acceptances was made more difficult by decisions of the Supreme Courts of Florida in 1926 and of Texas in 1927 ruling that the trade acceptance is not a negotiable instrument and so does not come under the provisions of the Uniform Negotiable Instruments Acts in force, at present, in all of the 48 states. The American Acceptance Council offered a revised standard form for the trade acceptance which would make its status as coming under the Act clear.

The fact that the use of the trade acceptance was somewhat increased between 1918 and 1920 is evident from Table 2. But after the decline which set in in 1921 and 1922, there was no real recovery in the extent to which this instrument was used. The propaganda for the trade acceptance was continued during 1923, it being argued that the time was auspicious because the time of recovery from a business depression was a time when a large volume of new debts were being contracted, thus rendering easier a change in methods of doing business. After 1923 the amount of trade acceptances taken by the Reserve banks declined steadily. In November, 1924, the *Acceptance Bulletin* published an article, "Are Trade Acceptances Gaining in Favor?" in which prominence was given to the reasons why they were not. This closed the active part of the early trade acceptance campaign.

The breakdown of business and the liquidation of credit which took place during 1932 started a new trade acceptance campaign. Buying for cash had been superseded, not by buying for credit, but by no buying at all. The Reserve banks embarked upon an extensive campaign of security buying in the open market but none of the funds thus released found their way to business via new loans. At the suggestion of Governor Meyer of the Federal Reserve Board, a committee of twelve business men and bankers was appointed by Governor Harrison of the Federal Reserve Bank of New York to examine into ways and means of promoting the extension of credit to trade and industry. As soon as this committee was announced, the American Acceptance Council saw the opportunity to advance its old favorite—the trade acceptance. The *Acceptance Bulletin* for May and June, 1932, carried editorials urging upon the committee the endorsement of this instrument. The committee accepted this suggestion and officially endorsed the trade acceptance, stating that its use would bring about further use of credit by business, and therefore business recovery. Much publicity followed this move lasting for a few weeks only. After this the subject was dropped and there has been no evidence that the use of the trade acceptance increased as a result of the statements made by the committee that large corporations had endorsed its use. It is difficult to see how any greater extensions of credit can take place by means of the trade acceptance than by any other plan of financing. It would appear that the result of such a campaign, if it were successful, would be a simple substitution of one credit instrument for another.

The Reserve banks have bought trade acceptances to such a limited extent in the open market that they cannot be said to have stimulated the use of this instrument, except through publicity methods. How ineffective all publicity in this connection has been has already been demonstrated. By their preference for the trade acceptance over the one name note, the Reserve banks have not directly injured the standing of one name commercial paper. But they have neglected an opportunity to improve and standardize it while there was still some in existence to improve and standardize.

Credit Analysis

Since so much emphasis had been placed upon the lack of uniformity of credit instruments before the passage of the Federal Reserve Act, the Board made an effort, in its first rulings and regulations, to lay down conditions on the filing of financial statements in connection with paper offered for rediscount.

Old Circular No. 13, issued November 10, 1914, required the filing of the borrower's financial statement with the member bank if the paper was offered for rediscount except for two name paper and paper showing on its face the character of the transaction out of which it arose.[8] While statements audited by a certified public accountant were not required, they were to be given under oath and to contain both balance sheets and profit and loss statements. They

[8] *Federal Reserve Bulletin*, 1914, pp. 182-184.

were also to be accompanied by a statement of the aggregate amount which the firm expected to borrow on short credit or sale of its paper.

Due to the complaints of bankers that borrowers were not accustomed to filing statements with loan applications and that considerable extra accounting work would be necessary to produce these statements at quick notice, the Board modified its requirements two months later. In Circular No. 3, issued January 25, 1915, it ruled that the requirement held for "purchased paper" only. But the fact that the Board hoped that the relaxation of the requirements would be temporary is indicated by its inclusion of the following statement in Circular No. 3:[9]

> While it has been thought best not to insist upon a written statement in the case of limited borrowings by depositors, when officers of member banks from their own personal knowledge certify to the eligibility of the paper offered for discount, it is urged, nevertheless, that member banks do their utmost to accustom their borrowers to furnishing such statements.

Regulation A, Series of 1916, covering requirements as to rediscounting paper under the terms of section 13 of the Federal Reserve Act required that financial statements should be on file with the member bank with respect to all notes offered for rediscount which had been purchased from sources other than a depositor or another member bank and for paper of one borrower aggregating more than 10 per-cent of the paid in capital of the member bank or $5,000. In the case of drafts, bills of exchange and trade acceptances, the ruling reads that the Federal Reserve bank "may require a recent financial statement of one or more of the parties to the instrument." This regulation has not been changed.

[9] *Federal Reserve Bulletin*, 1915, p. 37.

Regulation B, covering purchase in the open market of paper eligible under the terms of section 14 of the Federal Reserve Act, requires that financial statements be furnished only if the paper is not endorsed or accepted by a member bank.

Thus, it can be seen that the requirements of the Federal Reserve Board as to the filing of financial statements conform to the practice of the period before the Federal Reserve System was inaugurated. Open market commercial paper bought by member banks and offered for rediscount at Reserve banks is the only type of paper for which financial statements are consistently required. While the Board made some attempt in its first regulations to require statements for other kinds of paper, it was forced to give in to current practice, except in the case of paper of large denomination.

The Board has paid little attention to the actual analysis of the statements given, as it considers this to be the affair of the individual Reserve banks. In 1916 it ruled that it would merely pass upon the form of financial statements and that it would not be necessary for the statements themselves to prove satisfactory to the Board.[10] In 1917 it made its only ruling taking account of credit analysis in determining the eligibility of paper. It decided that if there is doubt as to the purpose for which a loan is to be made a statement showing a reasonable excess of quick assets over current liabilities may be taken as showing that the proceeds of the loan are to be used for a commercial purpose.[11] But this decision was reversed in a later ruling in which it was decided that the ratio of quick assets to current liabilities was not a test of eligibility. This ruling reads as follows:[12]

[10] *Federal Reserve Bulletin*, 1916, p. 13.

[11] *Federal Reserve Bulletin*, 1917, p. 527 (3).

[12] *Federal Reserve Bulletin*, 1921, p. 546.

It is not the present policy of the Federal Reserve Board to lay down definite tests for determining whether paper which is eligible for discount by Federal Reserve Banks as a matter of law should be considered acceptable for rediscount from a credit standpoint.

This ruling did give the individual Reserve banks the power to refuse to rediscount specific pieces of paper on the basis of their credit standing or of the credit standing of the bank applying for a loan.

In keeping with the desire of the Federal Reserve Board to pay more attention to the form than to the substance of financial statements, several Federal Reserve banks published model forms for statements in the early years of their existence. They have done nothing toward encouraging their use.

The Federal Reserve Board has determined to define paper as self-liquidating, if it conforms to the test of the specific transaction, either past or contemplated. While the Board did once rule that paper whose eligibility cannot be determined by this method might be considered to be self-liquidating if the financial statement of the concern is satisfactory, it has generally left the analysis of financial statements in the hands of the individual Reserve banks. The existence of collateral is taken account of in that the requirement that financial statements be on file is suspended in the case of paper secured by warehouse receipts covering readily marketable staples or by bonds and notes of the United States government.[18]

SUMMARY

It is apparent from this study that one name paper had become the means of extending credit to the most reliable borrowers before the passage of the Federal Reserve Act.

[18] *Regulation A, Series of 1928.*

While it is true that one name notes are seldom tied to specific transactions, the growing practice of credit analysis insured that current borrowings of business firms would be kept within the limits of their commercial dealings. Standards were highest in the case of open market commercial paper. In the case of one name notes used for direct bank borrowing the tendency to conform to the methods of the open market was growing. This tendency might have been encouraged by the Reserve banks. Instead of doing this, they embarked upon a futile campaign to change business methods by forcing the use of the trade acceptance upon the business community. They appear to have forgotten that credit instruments arise from the dealings of business firms with one another. The banks have to discount and the Reserve banks to rediscount what is brought to them. By choosing an instrument which has been used for poorer accounts and offering it a preferential position the Reserve banks encouraged a weak type of borrowing. It is the duty of banks to take the best paper offered in the form in which it is drawn. Since the Reserve banks have no direct control over business methods they resorted to publicity methods to accomplish their aim. The organization of dealers in trade acceptances gave them support but the campaign failed because it was an effort to encourage something which was not already in use, and, therefore, was not fully understood.

In defining the eligibility of paper for rediscount the Federal Reserve Act and the Federal Reserve Board have stated that it must be "self-liquidating" and that the test of the self-liquidating nature of paper shall be the specific transaction. The analysis of financial statements was left to the individual Reserve banks which were to determine from this analysis, not the eligibility of paper, but its acceptability from a credit standpoint.

CHAPTER V

The Bankers' Acceptance Market

The bankers' acceptance market in the United States is a recent innovation introduced by the Federal Reserve Act. It was created by Act of Congress. The market has continued in existence, not by virtue of the need for it, but on the basis of the support given it by the operations of the Federal Reserve banks in the open market. Therefore, any discussion of Federal Reserve policy must include a discussion of the attitude of the Reserve System toward the bankers' acceptance market. The process of credit recognition and the creation of immediate purchasing power by means of the bankers' acceptance is a roundabout process and therefore requires some explanation.

THE NATURE OF THE BANKERS' ACCEPTANCE

A bankers' acceptance closely resembles a trade acceptance in form, although the draft is accepted by a bank in the interest of the debtor, rather than by the debtor himself. It is particularly useful as an instrument of foreign trade where the buyers and sellers are not in close contact with one another and therefore are ignorant of each other's credit standing. In such cases buyers take letters of credit from their banks authorizing sellers of goods to draw upon the banks up to specified amounts and for definite purposes. Letters of credit vary in form, some of them imposing more limitations than others. The form of the letter of credit is not of interest in this discussion. It is the bankers' acceptance growing out of the letter of credit which adds to the circulating medium.

Bankers' acceptance credit differs from bank credit arising from loans and discounts in that the accepting bank assumes less immediate responsibility—that is, it does not increase its deposit liabilities. Where loans and discounts result in the substitution of a bank's demand liabilities for time or demand liabilities of borrowers, the acceptance of drafts by the same bank entails the substitution of the bank's time liabiiities for time liabilities of the borrowers with the same maturity. The borrowers agree to supply the bank with funds to meet the drafts before they are due. Consequently there is no immediate reason why accepting banks should not expand without limit by this means. In the case of direct bank loans the bank is deterred from overexpansion by fear of having to clear its deposits. The possibility that clients in whose favor drafts are accepted will not deposit funds to meet the maturing drafts is more remote and so is a less effective check to bank expansion. If drawers of drafts wish to increase their power to purchase goods immediately they must arrange for the discount of drafts which banks have accepted for them. In such cases discounting banks substitute for the time liabilities of accepting banks, represented by drafts, their own demand liabilities.

REASONS FOR INTRODUCING THE DOLLAR BANKERS' ACCEPTANCE

There had been two undesirable effects of the absence of authorization to accept in the United States. The first was the loss to American banks of a profitable source of business which carried little risk. Before the passage of the Federal Reserve Act most foreign trade of the country, both with England and with other foreign countries, was financed by means of sterling drafts. Considerations of nationalism led to a demand for their replacement by dollar drafts.

The second undesirable effect of the inability of American

banks to accept had to do with the consequence of the lack of dollar acceptances available in the American money markets upon bank portfolio policies, resulting in the use of bank funds in more speculative investments. Banks had been accustomed to investing their secondary reserves in brokers' call loans. The needs of brokers were considerations secondary to the availability of funds in determining the extent to which brokers borrowed. Violent fluctuations in security prices and in the volume of capital directed to industrial use were the result. The provision of a liquid credit instrument at an attractive yield was looked to to direct the secondary reserves of banks into a more useful form of investment. In order to give the banks a means of conversion of their secondary reserves into currency before the maturity of the bills held by them, it was hoped that regional discount markets would develop in Reserve bank cities.

THE REGULATION OF BANKERS' ACCEPTANCES IN THE UNITED STATES

It is desirable that bankers' acceptances possess great uniformity of quality to enhance their marketability. They are drawn only for the safest types of transactions and consequently are marketed at a low rate of interest. A transaction may be defined as safe if it satisfies one of two conditions. Either it must represent a sale of goods passing through the channels of trade between producer and consumer or it must be of such a nature that the goods representing the transactions may be stored so that the accepting bank may appropriate them. Both types of transactions have been used as a basis for bankers' acceptance credits. In the early years the Federal Reserve Act limited the use of acceptance credits to cases where there had been a sale of goods for foreign trade. Later on less emphasis was placed on the transaction and the secured draft came to take its place beside the draft based on a specific transaction.

Authorization to accept time bills of exchange was granted to national banks by a provision of section 13 of the Federal Reserve Act. Such bills were limited to those arising out of transactions involving the importation or exportation of goods and having not more than six months sight to run. In view of the fact that the accepting bank lends only a guarantee, the aggregate amount which any member bank might accept was limited to one-half of its paid up capital and unimpaired surplus.

Federal Reserve banks were permitted, by section 13, to rediscount acceptances of the kinds authorized for acceptance by member banks with a maturity of not more than three months and endorsed by a member bank. Under section 14, they were permitted to purchase such bills in the open market, with or without the endorsement of a member bank. The Board interpreted section 14 as permitting the purchase of acceptances based on imports and exports with a maturity up to six months.

On March 3, 1915, the Act was amended to permit the acceptance by member banks of bills up to an aggregate amount of 100 percent of their capital and surplus if they had previously been granted this privilege by the Federal Reserve Board.

On September 7, 1916, the purposes for which banks were allowed to accept drafts upon them were widened by an amendment to the Act. The domestic shipment draft was introduced, also the draft drawn against goods stored in warehouses, and the maturity of these drafts was limited to six months. They were to be fully secured by shipping documents or warehouse receipts at the time of acceptance. This change in the Act represented a departure from the previous practice of limiting the bankers' acceptance to credit transactions involving an actual sale of goods and substituting the secured draft. The aggregate amount of acceptance liability which a member bank might assume on account of these new types of drafts was limited to 50 percent of its paid up capital and unimpaired surplus.

Another type of bankers' acceptance authorized by the amendment to the Federal Reserve Act of September 7, 1916, not tied to a specific transaction, is the draft drawn by banks or bankers in foreign countries for the purpose of creating dollar exchange. The regulation of such acceptance powers was vested in the Federal Reserve Board and it has since then authorized them only in the cases of countries which it has named—principally located in South America. These drafts were intended to furnish the means of stabilizing the seasonal variations in the rates of exchange of the currencies of the countries which exported only one or a few crops.

The Federal Reserve Act made possible the bankers' acceptance. But the authorization in the Act applied to national banks only. State laws regarding acceptance powers of state banks and trust companies vary in their provisions, some of them conforming to the Federal Reserve Act, others being more liberal and still others making no authorization for acceptance by state banks.

The lack of any experience with bankers' acceptances in the United States made the Federal Reserve Board lay down rather definite rules in regulations, rulings and opinions of counsel regarding methods which member banks should follow in accepting them and as to methods which Federal Reserve banks should follow in discounting or purchasing them. Fear that member banks would accept drafts based on the shipment of goods between domestic points in order to provide manufacturers with working capital made the Board rule that they could not be made if their maturities exceeded the time required to finance the underlying transaction, provided this time did not exceed six months. Similarly the length of time a warehouse acceptance was to run was limited to "the time ordinarily necessary to effect a reasonably prompt sale, shipment, or distribution into the process of manufacture or consumption."[1]

Domestic shipment drafts were further limited by rulings of the Federal Reserve Board. In the early years an attempt was made to limit their use to the financing of shipments of goods that had been sold. In the case of a draft drawn by a purchaser of goods the maturity was limited to the time of shipment of the goods, whereas a draft drawn by the seller might have a maturity sufficient to cover sale as well as shipment, providing the terms of sale conformed to those customary in the trade.[2] In cases where there was no bona fide sale, as in a sale by a corporation to its agent, the maturity of the draft was to cover the time of shipment only.[3] In 1929 the Federal Reserve Board reversed these rulings by permitting domestic shipment acceptances, whether drawn by a buyer or by a seller, to be used to cover both shipment and sale.[4] This ruling was of great significance because it gave industry the right to raise working capital through the bankers' acceptance market and, because of the prominent part played in that market by the Reserve banks, based a part of Reserve bank credit upon the working capital needs of industry.

Domestic warehouse credits have assumed a more important place in the history of bankers' acceptances. When the amendment to the Federal Reserve Act of September 7, 1916, first authorized the acceptance by member banks of drafts secured by readily marketable staples stored in warehouses, it was feared that credit extended in this manner would be

[1] Regulations A and B, Series of 1920.

[2] *Federal Reserve Bulletin*, 1922, p. 52.

[3] *Federal Reserve Bulletin*, 1917, p. 690.

[4] *Federal Reserve Bulletin*, 1929, p. 811.

used to finance speculation in commodities. In order to prevent this misapplication of bank funds the Federal Reserve Board ruled that such credits should be used only where " the goods covered by the warehouse receipt are being held in storage pending reasonably immediate sale, shipment, or distribution into the process of manufacture." The same ruling declared a draft drawn for an indefinite period of time ineligible for acceptance by a member bank.[5] As no definition of the exact length of a definite period of time or of the meaning of the words " reasonably immediate " is given, it is difficult, on the basis of this ruling, to prevent the use of warehouse acceptances for purposes of speculation. Inasmuch as these acceptances are used to carry goods during those seasons of the year when prices are low due to the harvesting of crops, they are a legitimate form of bank credit. But the danger of abuse of such credits is very great. Until the Federal Reserve Board issues rulings on the exact seasons of the year at which acceptances based on specific kinds of staples may be made and the seasons when they must mature, it would seem advisable for the Reserve banks to avoid rediscounting them or purchasing them.

Further problems connected with the granting of warehouse acceptance credits are the nature of the warehouse in which the goods are stored and the nature of the goods which may be classed as " readily marketable staples." The former was the subject of a great number of rulings. A suitable warehouse is defined as one which is owned or leased independently of the owner of the goods and which does not permit the owner to have access to them. The latter was covered by the following definition: " A readily marketable staple may be defined as an article of commerce, agriculture, or industry of such uses as to make it the subject of constant dealings in ready markets with such frequent quotations of

[5] *Federal Reserve Bulletin*, 1919, p. 858 (2).

prices as to make (a) the price easily and definitely ascertainable and (b) the staple itself easy to realize upon by sale at any time." [6] Cattle could be treated as a readily marketable staple.[7] The passage of the Eighteenth Amendment introduced some complications in the case of liquors, which had formerly been considered to be readily marketable staples. It was decided that whiskey in bond, while a suitable form of collateral for a bank loan, could not be the basis of a bankers' acceptance and that sacramental wine had too limited a market to be considered a readily marketable staple.[8]

Bankers' acceptances based on goods stored in warehouses were at first assumed to apply to goods stored in domestic warehouses only. But General Counsel of the Board gave the opinion in 1919 that they might be used to cover goods stored in foreign countries if payable in the United States in dollars and that such drafts might be rediscounted by Reserve banks, though not purchased by them in the open market.[9] Regulation B, Series of 1923, admitted such paper to the privilege of purchase by Reserve banks while Regulations A and B, Series of 1923, removed the restriction that they be payable in the United States in dollars.[10]

The rulings and regulations as to bankers' acceptances based on imports and exports remained strict until 1927. As late as 1926 the Board ruled that national banks could accept drafts drawn upon them by other banks " against the security of import or export bills of exchange previously discounted by such other banks, provided that such drafts are drawn before the underlying import or export transactions are com-

[6] *Federal Reserve Bulletin*, 1919, p. 652.

[7] *Federal Reserve Bulletin*, 1918, p. 309.

[8] *Federal Reserve Bulletin*, 1920, p. 494, 1921, p. 419.

[9] *Federal Reserve Bulletin*, 1919, p. 740.

[10] Federal Reserve Board, *Annual Report*, 1923, pp. 266-271.

pleted." [11] A transaction involving merely the sale of goods within a foreign country was not considered by the Federal Reserve Board to involve importation or exportation.[12] In November, 1927, the Board ruled that " bankers' acceptances may properly be considered as growing out of transactions involving the importation or exportation of goods when drawn for the purpose of financing the sale and distribution on usual credit terms of imported or exported goods into the channels of trade, whether or not the bills are accepted after the physical importation or exportation has been completed." This ruling admitted such acceptances to Reserve bank portfolios as well as permitting their acceptance by member banks.[13]

THE BANKERS' ACCEPTANCE MARKET IN THE UNITED STATES

The Federal Reserve Act simply authorized the acceptance of time drafts by national banks—a privilege not accorded to them previously—and the rediscount or purchase of such accepted drafts by Federal Reserve banks. The establishment of a mechanism for marketing drafts after acceptance was left in the hands of private business.

The Dealers

In 1917 the Discount Corporation of New York was organized by a group of prominent accepting banks to deal in bankers' acceptances. Other dealers organized soon thereafter. In the early years there was so slight a demand from discounting banks that a market could not be said to have existed. The Federal Reserve banks assisted the dealers to market their bills by buying bills outright from them or by purchasing them under 15-day repurchase agreements.

[11] *Federal Reserve Bulletin*, 1926, pp. 854-855.

[12] *Federal Reserve Bulletin*, 1924, p. 638.

[13] *Federal Reserve Bulletin*, 1927, p. 860.

Drawers and endorsers of drafts have never become accustomed to marketing their own bills in the United States. Dealers generally buy directly from the accepting banks.

The second purpose of introducing the dollar bankers' acceptance into the money market—to give banks an outlet for their secondary reserves—can only be accomplished on a nation wide scale if dealers are scattered throughout the country. Therefore, some of the prominent dealers made attempts to establish branches in cities other than New York. But these branch offices either have been closed or have turned their attention to treasury bills. Centers in which there have in the past been markets are Boston, San Francisco, Cleveland, Fort Worth, Houston, and Philadelphia. Boston is the only one which survives. At present there are only eight dealers in bankers' acceptances, all of whom have their head offices in New York.[14]

The Accepting Banks

Acceptances of large New York banks are preferred in the market to those of out of town banks or smaller metropolitan banks. In fact, there are times when no other bills will be bought in large volume by any discounting banks than those of perhaps three to five large New York banks. Professor Beckhart estimated that from 70 to 80 percent of all acceptances are executed by banks in New York City at all times.[15]

[14] The dealers are the New York and Hanseatic Corporation, Salomon Bros. & Hutzler, The Discount Corporation of New York, The First of Boston Corporation, The Shawmut Corporation of Boston, The M. & T. Securities Corporation, Alexander T. Stephan and The Bankers' Discount Co.

[15] B. H. Beckhart, *The New York Money Market*, vol. iii, p. 333. The American Acceptance Council stated that for the last few years 40 of the first 100 accepting banks have been located in New York City, 7 in Boston, 6 each in Philadelphia and San Francisco, 5 in Chicago and 4 in Los Angeles. The remainder are scattered. In October, 1932, there

The Reserve banks themselves have encouraged the concentration of the businesses of accepting and dealing in bankers' acceptances in the hands of a small group of New York City banks and dealers by means of their Open Market Investment Committee (formerly the Open Market Policy Conference.) This committee buys bills in New York City for the account of out of town Reserve banks. The eleven

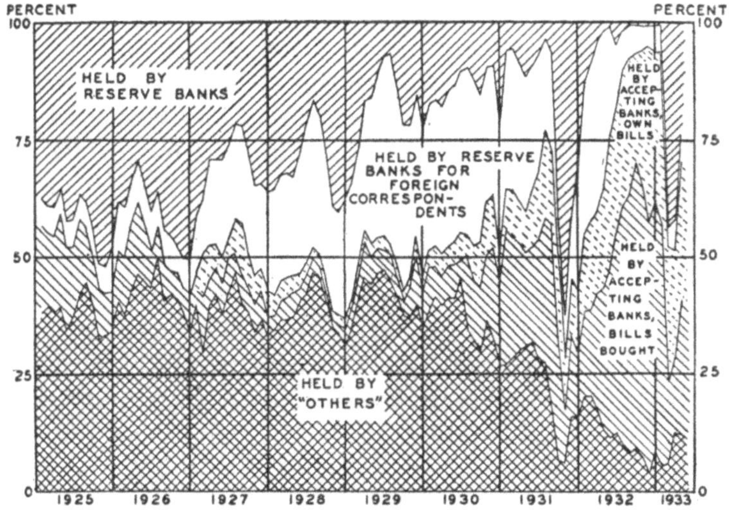

CHART 1. THE BANKERS' ACCEPTANCE MARKET
Data from the American Acceptance Council

other Reserve banks have tended more and more to buy their bills through the committee and less and less to buy them directly from banks in their own localities.[16] Foreign

were only 118 accepting banks in the United States. The number has declined greatly since the banking holiday of March, 1933. *Acceptance Bulletin*, November, 1932, p. 1, and April, 1933, pp. 1-3.

[16] Most of the Reserve banks gave information as to the source of bankers' acceptances which they purchased during each month from 1922 through 1930 to the Senate Committee on Banking and Currency.

funds going into the bankers' acceptance market are for the most part invested by the Federal Reserve Bank of New York.[17] These tendencies have strengthened the position of New York and weakened the positions of outside cities, from the point of view both of the establishment of dealers and of the encouragement of accepting by local banks.

Discounting Banks

In the past a large part of the creation of immediately available bank credit through the discount of bankers' acceptances has consisted in Reserve bank credit. Chart 1 shows the distribution of bankers' acceptances outstanding as reported to the American Acceptance Council between different types of investors.

During the first four years for which data are available the Reserve banks supported the bankers' acceptance market to so great an extent that this means was used to contribute to the current inflation of credit based on Reserve bank credit. Beginning in 1928 when the French franc was stabilized and a large volume of French funds were put out at interest in New York, foreign banks supplied the funds to support the American bill market. It was not until 1930 that American banks began discounting bills with their own funds. After this the Reserve banks have stepped in only in times of great stringency—in the fall of 1931 and again just before the banking holiday of March, 1933.

The decline in the amount held by " others including dealers " shown on Chart 2 indicates a decrease in the holdings of banks other than accepting banks. The member bank call

Tables of these, published in *Hearings Pursuant to S. Res. 71*, appendix, part 6, pp. 886-898, indicate an increase in the purchases through the committee during that period.

[17] Some foreign banks invest in bills which are ineligible for discount at or purchase by Reserve banks. These bills are few in number and are never marketed to American banks.

reports sent to the Federal Reserve Board indicate that at the end of 1928 all member banks held 212 million dollars' worth of purchased acceptances while only 49 million dollars' worth were held by the group of accepting banks. By the end of 1932 the amount held by all member banks was 405 million dollars' worth, the group of accepting banks holding 380 million dollars' worth.

CHANGES IN THE VOLUME OF BANKERS' ACCEPTANCES OUTSTANDING

During the period for which monthly data are available,[18] the period since December, 1924, the volume of bankers' acceptances increased substantially, reaching a peak at the end of 1929. At that date there were more than twice as many bills outstanding as at the end of 1924. After 1929 the decline was rapid. At the beginning of the period under consideration most of the bills drawn were for exports and imports. There was a gradual increase in the use of domestic warehouse acceptances continuing until 1932 and a very rapid increase in the use of foreign storage and shipment acceptances. In 1933 these two classes of bills together accounted for more than half of the bankers' acceptances outstanding. This change in the make up of the acceptance liabilities of banks reflects the more liberal rulings of the Federal Reserve Board, permitting greater latitude in the use of such drafts for financing the holding of goods off markets.

[18] The American Acceptance Council receives reports from all of the accepting banks on the volume of their acceptance liabilities at the end of the month. Since December, 1924, these reports have been received monthly. They were made occasionally before that date—March 31, 1920 through 1924, and at the end of every year. The reports of condition of member banks on call dates give the total acceptance liabilities of these banks. The data of the American Acceptance Council are more inclusive, due to the fact that many drafts are accepted by specialized acceptance corporations—particularly the International Acceptance Bank, recently merged with the Bank of the Manhattan Co., which is one of the banks reporting to the American Acceptance Council.

Bankers' Acceptances Based on Imports and Exports

These bills, sometimes picturesquely called " salt water bills," represented the bulk of the bankers' acceptances in the market for the first decade of the Federal Reserve System's operation. They still represent a large proportion of those outstanding. The amount of such paper in the market at any time is ruled by (1) the amount of export and import trade of the United States, (2) the relative attractiveness of financing such transactions in London or in New York and (3) the length of time which the average bill runs. Other factors remaining the same, if the maturity of the average bill is lengthened, more bills will be outstanding at any time as a result of a given value of past export or import transactions.

Chart 2, showing a comparison between United States exports and imports and the acceptances based on these transactions, illustrates the close relationship between these factors. Between October, 1926, and the end of 1928 the volume of export acceptances outstanding increased relatively to the value of goods exported from the United States. If this relative rise was due to a shift of financing from London banks to New York banks, the cause did not lie in the favorable rate of interest. During the period, 1925 to 1927, when export acceptances outstanding in the United States were low compared to the volume of exports, the rate of interest on such paper in London averaged 0.55 percent above the rate in New York. For the three years, 1928 through 1930, the London rate averaged only 0.13 percent above the New York rate, yet there was a marked increase in the number of bankers' acceptances based on exports outstanding in New York in the later period.

It will be remembered that the Federal Reserve Board made a ruling in November, 1927, which had the effect of lengthening the period before maturity for export and import acceptances. Since this ruling came as a result of pressure by American exporters, it is probable that the length of export bills had been increasing before that time. After No-

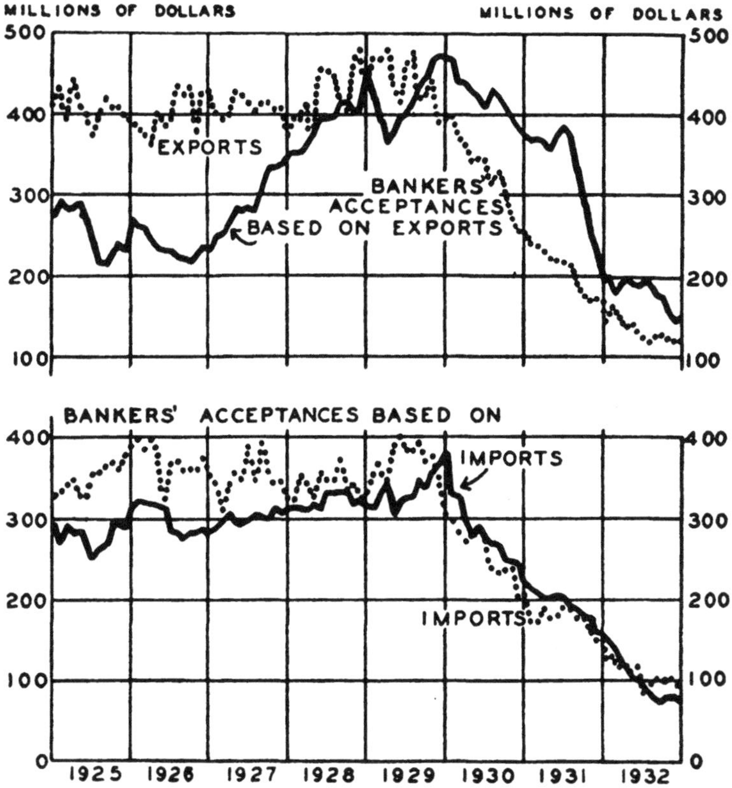

CHART 2. BANKERS' ACCEPTANCES BASED ON IMPORTS AND EXPORTS
Imports and Exports from United States Department of Commerce
Bankers' Acceptances Outstanding from American Acceptance Council
Data, adjusted for seasonal variation

vember, 1927, the maturity of export bills was again put forward and a larger and larger volume of bills remained outstanding as a result of any given volume of export transactions. In the case of import transactions, there was less pressure to lengthen terms of financing and so the curve of the volume of bankers' acceptances outstanding based on imports paralleled the imports curve. In the period of liquidation following 1929 the bankers' acceptance credits lagged behind the exports because of the long period which the bills had to run. But the decline after the date of the European financial crisis of July, 1931, was steep indicating that shorter terms prevailed after that. In the case of import credits, the liquidation was more prompt, showing that credit terms were shorter.

The successful liquidation of bankers' acceptances based on imports and exports in proportion to the decline in the volume of foreign trade attests to their essential liquidity.

The volume of exports and imports varies with the seasons, and the volume of bankers' acceptances based on export and import transactions, as would be expected, shows a corresponding variation with a time lag of from one to two months. Chart 3 shows that a low point in the volume of

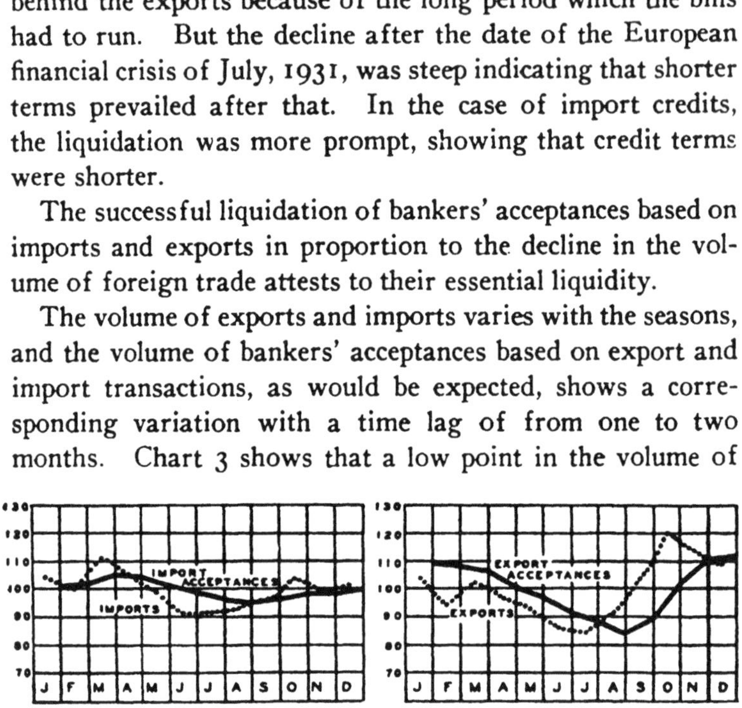

CHART 3. SEASONAL VARIATIONS IN BANKERS' ACCEPTANCES BASED ON IMPORTS AND EXPORTS
Data from same sources as Chart 2

exports is reached each year in the month of July, while the corresponding low point in export credits occurs at the end of August. The minor seasonal rise in exports between February and March of each year is not reflected in like degree in the amount of bills based on exports because the decline in exports between January and February and consequent rise from February to March is due to the fact that the number of days in February on which exporting can take place is about ten percent less than in January or March.

The seasonal variation in import credits and in imports, shown on Chart 3, indicate some relationship, though a less exact one than in the case of exports. The low month for imports into the United States is June. Acceptances based on imports do not reach their lowest point until the end of August. The high points in both imports and import acceptances are in March. When allowance is made for the effect on imports of the short month of February the two curves show a similar shape though the time lag between changes in import totals and consequent changes in import acceptances is a variable one. The reasons for the lack of regularity in the relationship are to be found in the type of imports into the country, the terms upon which these imports are financed and the type of organization doing the importing. Whereas exports are largely basic commodities being exported through the agency of large business combinations, imports consist for the most part in heterogeneous articles destined for final consumption. Large combinations have access to the bankers' acceptance market, where rates are low, whereas the small scale jobbers, retailers, etc., who do the importing, frequently must raise funds by other means.

Domestic Shipment and Warehouse Acceptances

Bankers' acceptances based on goods shipped between domestic points, shown on Chart 4, have constituted a very small proportion of the total volume of bankers' acceptances outstanding. The liberalized ruling of 1929, permitting the use of these bills for purposes of raising working capital, was followed by some increase in the volume outstanding during 1930 and 1931.

For the period of time for which data on the amount of domestic warehouse credits have been available, we may note from Chart 4 that they have displayed two movements, one of a seasonal nature and the other a growth evidently caused by the desire of holders of these goods to keep them off the market as their price declined. The seasonal movement was marked, indicating that the majority of these credits were liquid. But the gradual growth of the curve, shown on Chart 4, after 1929 is an indication that warehouse bankers' accept-

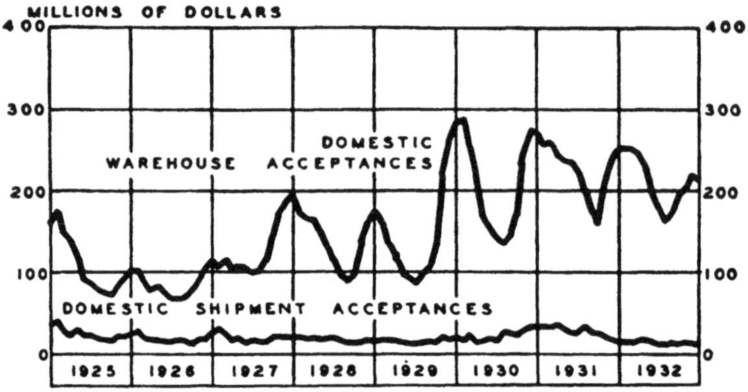

CHART 4. DOMESTIC SHIPMENT AND WAREHOUSE ACCEPTANCES
Data from American Acceptance Council

ance credits were used to hold goods off the market during a time when commodity prices were falling. Had the credits been liquid, the period of falling prices would have been a period of declining demand for bankers' acceptance accommodation.

Bankers' Acceptances Based on Goods Stored in or Shipped Between Foreign Countries

The dollar bankers' acceptance based on goods stored in or shipped between foreign countries, while permitted since 1919, did not appear in the market until February, 1925. At the end of that month 14 million dollars' worth of bankers' acceptances based upon foreign storage and shipment were in existence. This amount increased at the beginning of 1926. After July, 1927, the upward movement became precipitous, reaching a peak of more than 560 million dollars at the end of 1930. The upward movement became particularly pronounced after the middle of 1929. The decline was not very great until July, 1931, the date of the European

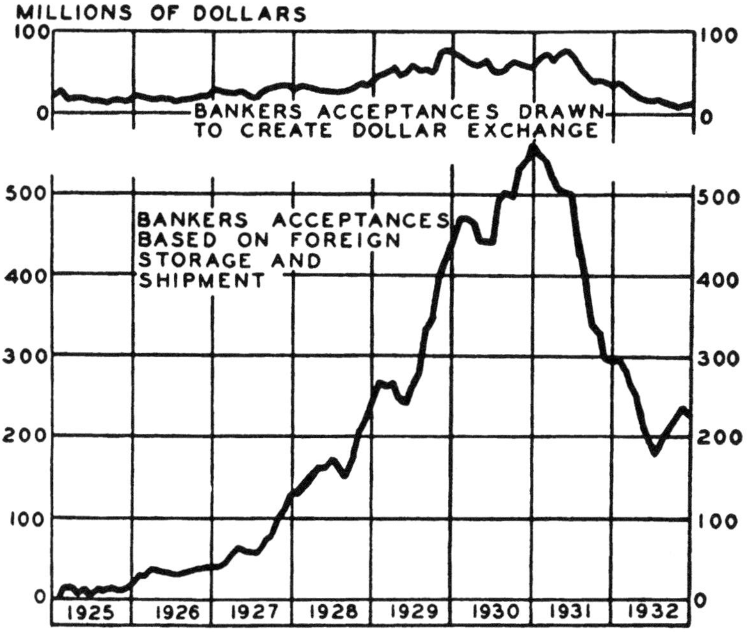

CHART 5. FOREIGN STORAGE AND SHIPMENT ACCEPTANCES AND DOLLAR EXCHANGE ACCEPTANCES
Data from American Acceptance Council

financial crisis. It was still over 200 million dollars in the summer of 1933. Foreign storage and shipment acceptances are shown on Chart 5.

In order to determine the cause of this extraordinary rise in acceptance credit extended to foreigners, we must make some study of the foreign trade of the United States. Estimates for the principal constituents of the entire balance of payments of the United States for each year beginning in 1922 through 1931 are available in a publication of the Department of Commerce, *The United States Balance of International Payments.* The tables are expressed as credit items less debit items, the balance being prefixed by a plus sign when payment is due to the United States and by a minus sign when payment is due by the United States.

TABLE 3

VISIBLE AND INVISIBLE ITEMS IN THE TRADE OF THE UNITED STATES EXCLUDING MOVEMENTS OF CAPITAL, PAYMENTS OF INTEREST AND DIVIDENDS, AND CURRENCY MOVEMENTS

(millions of dollars)

	1922	*1923*	*1924*	*1925*	*1926*	*1927*	*1928*	*1929*	*1930*	*1931*
Commodity trade ...	+702	+206	+882	+633	+278	+583	+865	+648	+801	+369
Tourist expenditures	—305	—280	—373	—410	—406	—444	—617	—638	—605	—458
Freights	—79	—83	—64	—84	—75	—66	—32	—66	—96	—72
Immigrant remittances	—255	—229	—229	—235	—218	—206	—218	—223	—166	—163
Charity and missionary contributions..	—75	—70	—55	—50	—46	—49	—51	—49	—49	—39
Miscellaneous	0	—9	+15	+13	+25	+45	—33	—67	—29	—41
Total..........	—12	—465	+176	—133	—462	—137	—86	—395	—144	—404

TABLE 4

PAYMENTS OF INTEREST ON DEBTS AND OF PRINCIPAL OF DEBTS PREVIOUSLY CONTRACTED CORRECTED FOR PAYMENTS OF INTEREST AND DIVIDENDS TO FOREIGN HOLDERS OF AMERICAN SECURITIES

(millions of dollars)

	1922	*1923*	*1924*	*1925*	*1926*	*1927*	*1928*	*1929*	*1930*	*1931*
Net dividend and interest payments ...	+411	+414	+443	+460	+472	+519	+537	+565	+616	+548
War debt receipts principal and interest	+158	+259	+183	+186	+195	+206	+207	+207	+241	+113
Total..........	+569	+673	+626	+646	+667	+725	+744	+772	+857	+661
Balance from Table 3	—12	—465	+176	—133	—462	—137	—86	—395	—144	—404
Net total to be settled by gold or by loans	+557	+208	+802	+513	+205	+588	+658	+377	+713	+257

TABLE 5

THE EXTENT TO WHICH FOREIGN OBLIGATIONS TO THE UNITED STATES WAS COVERED BY LONG TERM LOANS AND GOLD OR CURRENCY MOVEMENTS WITH THE BALANCE WHICH WAS COVERED BY SHORT TERM LOANS

(millions of dollars)

	1922	1923	1924	1925	1926	1927	1928	1929	1930	1931
Balance from Table 4	+557	+208	+802	+513	+205	+588	+658	+377	+713	+257
Gold and currency ..	−194	−245	−236	+72	−72	+154	+272	−120	−256	+166
Long term private capital movement..	−753	+30	−733	−560	−540	−695	−718	−319	−295	+218
Total	−390	−7	−167	+25	−407	+47	+212	−62	+162	+641
Errors and omissions	+15	+4	−49	+36	+48	−47	+14	+49	+323	+124
Total	−375	−3	−216	+61	−359	0	+226	−13	+485	+765
Balance, loaned at short term	+375	+3	+216	−61	+359	0	−226	+13	−485	−765

Bankers' acceptance credits of this type were used to pay for the export of goods from the United States at a time when foreign countries were not able to supply the means of settlement through their own exports to this country or through the proceeds of long term loans floated in this country.

Table 3 indicates that, in spite of the continuous existence of a favorable balance of commodity trade, the government and the people of the United States have owed money to foreigners on account of non-capital transactions every year since 1922 except for the year 1924. The extent to which this unfavorable balance was absorbed in payments of interest on debts due to the government and the people of the United States, payments of the principal of previously contracted debts, profits on properties held abroad by Americans, etc., is shown on Table 4. The existence of a continuously growing amount due to Americans on this account changes the picture. Every year a net balance was due to the United States. This has been paid by an application of the proceeds of long and short term loans floated in the United States and, to some extent, by gold. Table 5 shows the variability of that part of the payment which was met from the proceeds of foreign loans.

To connect foreign trade movements with the bankers' acceptance problem, one must first see how deficits in the balance of payments of the United States were covered during the years when the bankers' acceptance based on transactions taking place entirely within the borders of foreign countries was not yet in use, in other words, in the years before 1925. From Table 4 it is noted that the year 1922 was one in which a large amount of money was due to the United States to cover payments for goods and for debt services. This was met by payments to us of gold and by foreign long term securities floated in the United States. The year 1923 was one when the sale of foreign long term bonds met with difficulties. In fact there was a net balance due to the United States when the outflow of capital at long term is corrected for the influence of American long term securities bought by foreigners. Foreigners appear to have ceased depositing additional money here at short term or on call because the amount due on that account fell from 375 million dollars to only 3 million dollars. The result of this stoppage in the flow of long term capital abroad was an immediate contraction in our export trade, which had a favorable balance of only 206 million dollars as against 702 million dollars in 1922. In 1924 a renewal of foreign long term borrowing in American markets resulted in a favorable balance of commodity trade of 882 million dollars. The next year, 1925, saw a slight shrinkage in both foreign long term borrowing in the American market and the favorable balance of commodity trade. The effect of long term loan transactions on foreign trade in commodities in the years before the foreign bankers' acceptance had come into use was one of rapid readjustment.

In the last quarter of 1927 bankers' acceptances outstanding based on foreign transactions reached 100 million dollars in amount. From that time on the rise was steady and rapid. In 1928 short term credits granted by Americans to foreigners as well as long term bonds floated here increased rapidly. The proceeds of these loans were used to pay for goods exported from the United States and debt services and there was still a balance which was withdrawn in gold. In the following year, while short term credits granted to foreigners increased rapidly, as is shown by the increase in bankers' acceptances based on foreign storage and shipment, there was a net inflow of short term funds due to the attraction of the high call loan rate ruling in New York throughout the major part of the year. In spite of considerable falling off of loans resulting from foreign bond flotations in the United States, the favorable balance of export trade continued and was paid for only in part by gold shipped to this country. Had it not been for the readiness of American banks to grant foreigners credit in the form of acceptances, there would have been a large net inflow of foreign funds into the New York market and the huge balance of export trade could not have been maintained. In 1930 there was a further decline in foreign bond flotations. Despite this, foreign countries were supplied with funds with which to meet debt payments and to increase their imports from the United States by means of the abnormally large increase in bankers' acceptance credits granted to them. The way was paved for the numerous defaults of foreign bonds and the necessity of both a moratorium on intergovernmental debts and a freezing of short term bank credits in Germany which took place in 1931. The effect of a stoppage of long term loans on the balance of commodity trade was put off from 1929, the year in which the first great reduction in the amount loaned by means of bond issues occurred, until 1932 by means of a substitution of acceptance credit for long term loans.

The fact that foreign storage and shipment acceptances were illiquid is attested to by the fact that a large number were tied up in the standstill agreement consummated between German banks and American banks in 1931. The total of all kinds of short term loans involved was 5,360,000,000 Reichsmarks (about $1,175,000,000.) Of this a large part was in the form of bankers' acceptances.[19]

There appears to be conclusive proof that bankers' acceptances, supposedly the most liquid form of short term credit and, therefore, one recommended as an investment for secondary reserves of banks, were misused through the overissue of those based on goods stored in or shipped between foreign countries. These bills were used as substitutes for long term loans and their proceeds were applied, not to self-liquidating ventures, but to uses for which long term loans would have been the only suitable form of financing. When the American public became unwilling to buy long term foreign bonds in 1929, short term bank credit should not have been allowed to take their place. The effect of a stoppage of long term lending transactions on the export trade of the United States would then have been felt at an earlier time and the problem of recovery would have been simplified.

The questionnaire submitted by a sub-committee of the Banking and Currency Committee of the United States Senate to the Federal Reserve banks in 1930 included a question as to whether the increase in acceptances based on foreign

[19] The share of this represented by credits due to the Chase National Bank, head office, was $43,957,281, of which $25,762,025 represented acceptance credits and $17,195,256 represented cash loans. No other group has given us any figures on the amount involved. Therefore, we can only surmise that, since more than half of the Chase National Bank's share was in the form of acceptances, more than half of the total may have been also. There were other illiquid acceptance credits granted to Germany which were not included in the standstill agreement. *Annual Report to the Stockholders of the Chase National Bank*, statement of A. H. Wiggin, *Commercial and Financial Chronicle*, Jan. 16, 1932, p. 449.

storage and shipment was to be explained by the curtailment of capital exports to Central Europe in 1929. The replies to this question indicate that most of the Reserve banks had no comprehension of the true nature of the foreign acceptance. They explained it either as a healthy and normal development or as a shift of this type of business to New York from London caused by the high rates prevailing in the London market in the latter half of 1929. They thought it to be a normal way of financing export trade. Why acceptances based on export transactions were not found sufficiently satisfactory for that purpose they left unexplained. Only the Federal Reserve Bank of Chicago recognized the true nature of what was going on and its fundamental unsoundness. It stated: [20]

With regard to the large increase in the volume of acceptances drawn for foreign storage and shipment between foreign countries, it appears that a substantial amount of this business originates in Germany and other central European countries and that it results at least to some extent from a continued shortage of capital and is not likely to be reduced until long-term loans can be floated in this country or in London or Paris.

Bankers' Acceptances Payable in Foreign Currencies

Drafts drawn on American banks and accepted by them may, under the terms of Regulations A and B, Series of 1923, be drawn payable in foreign currencies. Such drafts are dependent for ultimate payment upon the stability of the currency in which they are drawn. Since the American Acceptance Council reports only the amount of dollar acceptances outstanding, we have no estimate of how many such drafts are accepted by American banks. We may only estimate their importance from the volume bought by Federal Reserve banks. This figure, translated into dollar values, indicates that the Reserve banks' holdings amounted, in nor-

[20] *Hearings Pursuant to S. Res. 71*, part 6, appendix, p. 853.

mal times, to around one million dollars' worth. But at times of stress in the international exchange markets, they often increased rapidly. In June, July and August, 1927, the pressure on foreign currencies caused a rise to close to 14 million dollars' worth. When low interest rates in this country brought about an easing of foreign exchange rates, they were paid off and the amount held by Reserve banks returned to the former level, actually standing very much below that in the summer of 1928. Toward the end of the speculative boom, in September and October, 1929, there was another increase, this time to a little less than 18 million dollars' worth. The liquidation to the normal one million was rapid in November. The next rise was in October, 1930—a time when gold was being imported into the United States. This condition lasted only about five months, although the total outstanding at the end of the month was slightly over 36 million dollars in January, 1931. After January there was another rapid contraction to normal. But the central European crisis of July, 1931, caused another rapid expansion in the amount of such drafts bought by Reserve banks. From only 1,073 thousand dollars at the end of May, they rose rapidly to 145,215 thousand dollars at the end of August. The bulk of this amount was liquidated during the period when the dollar was under pressure in the fall of 1931, though more than 30 million dollars' worth were illiquid enough to remain outstanding until March, 1933, when the flight of American capital supplied the means of liquidating all but 6 million dollars' worth.

Bankers' Acceptances Drawn to Furnish Dollar Exchange

This type of bankers' acceptance was first authorized in order to stabilize the foreign exchange rates of certain countries whose export trade depended upon a few products which were seasonal in their nature. It was expected that these purely finance bills, backed as they were by no actual commercial transactions, would be drawn during slack seasons when there were no exports and retired at the end of these seasons out of the proceeds of export bills paid. In this case, their amount should bear some relation to the prices of the principal products of those countries where they are used. The rise in the amount outstanding late in 1929 and again in the middle of 1931 shown on Chart 5, leads us to believe that they were used to attempt to stabilize exchange rates which showed a tendency at times to fall, not due to seasonal factors, but due to faults in the monetary structures of the countries where they were drawn. Like bankers' acceptances based on foreign storage and shipment, they were used as substitutes for long term loans.

THE RESERVE BANKS AND THE BANKERS' ACCEPTANCE MARKET

The Reserve banks have had complete control of the open market rate ruling in the bankers' acceptance market. In altering their acceptance buying rates, the Reserve banks have not altered the willingness of borrowers to use this market, but rather the willingness of the market to sell acceptances to the Reserve banks with a consequent readjustment of market rates to the Federal Reserve rate. Purchases of bankers' acceptances by the Federal Reserve Bank of New York for the account of foreign banks are made at a rate slightly below the official buying rate and varying with the latter. Consequently, at times when the market depends upon the Reserve banks for support, these institutions may be buying, not for their own, but for foreign account.

Chart 6 shows a comparison of the buying rate on bankers' acceptances of the Federal Reserve Bank of New York with the open market rate ruling in New York City, compared to the proportion of the total amount outstanding held by

Federal Reserve banks for their own and for foreign accounts. The upper lines, showing the rate at which such bills are bought by the Reserve Bank and by other purchasers,

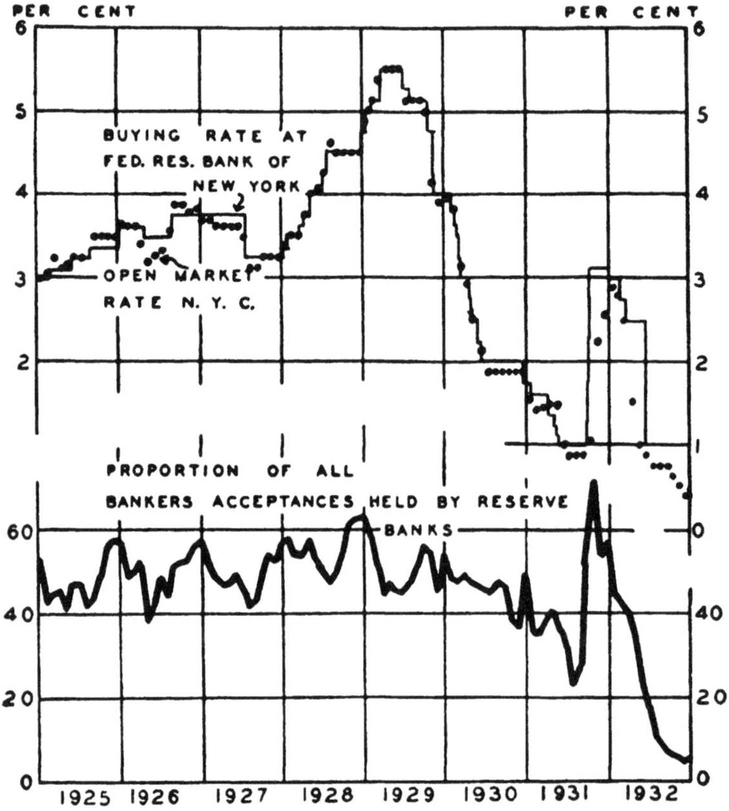

CHART 6. THE BANKERS' ACCEPTANCE RATE

Data on rates of interest from Federal Reserve Board.
Data on proportion of bankers' acceptances held by Federal Reserve banks computed from data of American Acceptance Council

closely parallel one another. The buying rate of the Federal Reserve Bank of New York can never remain more than a small fraction of one percent below the market rate for long, because such a situation would result in the bringing of more bills to the Reserve banks for purchase. It may be above the outside rate, in which case the bulk of bills sold are sold to outside investors. In such a case, the Reserve banks are resorted to in temporary periods of stringency.

The Reserve banks definitely intend to carry the seasonal load of the acceptance market, freeing the funds of discounting banks for other purposes. There is a pronounced seasonal movement in the volume of bankers' acceptances outstanding—the shape of the seasonal curve depending upon the type of transaction underlying the acceptance. All reach their low points at the end of July or August of each year. Domestic shipment acceptances and acceptances based on exports are at their maximum at the end of the year. Those based on imports rise until the end of March, while dollar exchange drafts are at their maximum at the end of January. There is no visible seasonal variation in acceptances based on goods stored in or shipped between foreign countries. The Reserve bank holdings of bankers' acceptances vary with the seasons in the same manner as do the total amounts of bankers' acceptances outstanding, but the change from the low point in the summer to the high point at the end of the year is far more steep. The data on which these conclusions are based are shown in Appendix I.

Reserve bank purchases of bankers' acceptances may be undertaken merely to stabilize the acceptance market or as a method of releasing Federal funds to be used as bank reserves. Purchases of the former class are typified by the seasonal policy of the Reserve banks. But purchases of the latter class—except in periods of great stress such as 1931 and 1933—may serve to provide commercial banks with reserves upon which to expand their loan portfolios.

During the summers of 1928 and 1929, although the Reserve banks had embarked upon restrictive credit policies, their buying rates on acceptances were held so low that these institutions absorbed more than the customary seasonal excess of bills. In both years loans to brokers for the account of New York City banks rose, showing that the Reserve bank purchases of bankers' acceptances had an inflationary effect.

Proper acceptance buying policy of the Reserve banks requires that their buying rates be kept consistently a little above the open market rate on the same kind of paper. In that case, the unloading of bankers' acceptances upon Reserve banks will take place only in times of emergency, when banks are not increasing their loans for other reasons. The possibility of Reserve bank credit released through the purchase of bankers' acceptances being used as a base for the extension of illiquid credit will be minimized.

RELATIVE SUCCESS OR FAILURE OF OBJECTIVES OF ACCEPTANCE POLICY

The intention of the framers of the Federal Reserve Act to build up a number of discount markets in Reserve bank cities has failed to materialize although there is an active market in New York. For the first fifteen years of Federal Reserve operation the willingness of the Reserve banks to buy acceptances in unlimited quantities prevented the use of this market as an outlet for secondary reserves of banks. Since that time Reserve bank buying rates have been held slightly above market rates on bankers' acceptances and banks have bought bills with a view to turning them into currency by sale to Reserve banks at times of stringency. Their success with this policy in October, 1931, and again in February, 1933, and the rapidity with which the member banks again undertook to carry the burden of discounting acceptances should be a recommendation of that policy. There is some hope that large metropolitan banks may invest their secondary reserves in bankers' acceptances. Unless out of town Reserve banks buy all of their bills locally there is no prospect that outside markets will develop.

The purely nationalistic aim of establishing the bankers' acceptance market in the United States—to finance foreign trade at home—has been a partial success. It is known that some of the foreign trade of the United States is still financed in London. But the dollar bankers' acceptance has come to stay. It is unfortunate that, in its haste to establish the dollar bankers' acceptance, the Federal Reserve Board has permitted these bills to be used to finance transactions not foreseen at the time when the Act was passed. Import and export bills have represented the best credit risks and have responded most to changes in trade. Warehouse credits—particularly foreign warehouse credits—have been misused. By their very nature they are fitted for use for speculative purposes. If granted in large amounts they will bring about a decline in the confidence of bankers in the dollar acceptance as an investment, and will prevent the establishment of a permanent discount market.

CHAPTER VI

Brokers' Loans and Federal Reserve Policy

THE POSITION OF THE FEDERAL RESERVE SYSTEM IN THE MARKET

The Federal Reserve System officially holds itself aloof from dealings in security loans. Yet with the exception of loans secured by bonds or notes of the United States government, its broader rate and credit policies have frequently been dictated with a view to influencing the total volume of such advances by other credit agencies in the country. In addition to this, the operations of the System have for a long time had an undesired and possibly an unexpected influence upon the volume of loans secured by stocks and bonds made by the commercial banks and other credit agencies.

The Federal Reserve banks may not deal directly in security markets, nor may they make loans for the purpose of enabling others to carry on such transactions. But they may deal in the long term market for bonds of the United States government. The open market powers of the Reserve banks in this respect have been described in Chapter II and some of the dealings have been summarized in Chapter III. The effects of Federal Reserve policies on security markets have been indirect and have grown out of a circumvention of certain policies of the System by the financial community. At times when Federal Reserve policies have been dictated with a view to affecting rates of interest, commercial banks have altered their loan policies with respect to loans on stocks and bonds with a consequent reaction on the stock and bond markets themselves.

The New York call loan renewal rate, or the rate at which the majority of brokers borrow, is sensitive to rate changes in the open money markets. Thus, policies of the Reserve System may alter the price paid by brokers for their accommodations. The effect of this rate on the amount borrowed is somewhat intricate. At times a low call loan rate has stimulated security speculation with borrowed funds. At times a high rate has not restricted borrowing but has attracted funds from other sources to an already over-active security market. At other times low call loan rates have been accompanied by almost complete stagnation in the markets for long term securities. How these apparent contradictions have resulted from Federal Reserve policies which had other aims in view than changes in the rate of security speculation will be demonstrated in this chapter.

TYPES OF SECURITY LOANS

Speculators or investors may finance themselves by borrowing from their banks or by borrowing from stock brokers, who in turn borrow from banks. The former operation leaves the borrower in a more secure position in case of temporary declines in the price of stocks. Banks theoretically have the right to sell securities held against all loans, on failure to repay on demand or at maturity, or when their market values decline below the values of the loans. In practice they do not always do so. Brokers, on the other hand, always sell the collateral of their customers when its market value falls below its loan value. In fact, the New York Stock Exchange rulings contain an exhortation to that effect.[1] Still, there are certain advantages in favor of

[1] *Rules Adopted by the Governing Committee Pursuant to the Constitution of the New York Stock Exchange*, Section 1, chap. xii. "The

borrowing from a broker. A customer deposits his margin and puts in his order to buy and the transaction is completed as far as he is concerned. At a bank he must previously have established a " line of credit " by the maintenance of a good deposit balance for some time. The transaction is further complicated by the necessity of producing the securities before the loan is closed. The bank may also ask for a certain type of collateral or for mixed collateral consisting of an assortment of stocks or bonds. The broker holds the customer's securities after they are bought. When he in turn wishes to borrow, he can produce the mixed collateral from the securities bought by his many customers. For these reasons there is normally a difference between the type of borrower applying for credit extension to a broker and the type applying to a bank. The former are either men of smaller means or those carrying on purely speculative transactions with a rapid turnover. The latter are likely to be investors who buy in anticipation of the receipt of income and intend to hold their securities for some time. Nevertheless, the similarity of the terms ruling on the two markets results in a considerable shifting of loans from one to the other.

SOURCES AND USES OF FUNDS IN THE SECURITY LOAN MARKETS

Uses of Funds

Bank loans on security collateral are frequently applied to the carrying of securities, although they are used for a variety of other purposes. Answers to a questionnaire sent to 30 commercial banks—10 in New York City and 20 scattered throughout the country—by a sub-committee of the Committee on Banking and Currency of the United States

acceptance and carrying of an account for a customer, whether a member or a non-member, without adequate margin, may constitute an act detrimental to the interest or welfare of the Exchange."

Senate in 1930 prove that the majority of collateral loans are used for the purpose of carrying securities.[2] In the case of loans used for other purposes, had they not been made, the underlying securities might have been sold. Therefore, these loans serve indirectly as well as directly for the purpose of carrying stocks and bonds.

The total of brokers' loans has been shown to bear a close relationship to the prices of securities traded in on the New York Stock Exchange, changing somewhat after these.[3] But the fact of this time lag has been shown by Professor Beckhart to convey no information as to a causal sequence. He states, " Proceeding from a deductive point of view, an increase in stock prices must arise from a demand made effective through savings or through present or future reliance on credit." [4] Therefore, we cannot dismiss the role of the supply of funds as a determinant of the volume of new purchasing power directed to speculative use, thus excusing the Federal Reserve System from any responsibility for the growth of brokers' loans. The sequence is rather that of readily available money followed by security purchases made on the basis of credit which is expected to be recognized and a credit transaction entered into the day after the security purchase is made.

[2] Tables of the proportion of security loans estimated to have been made for commercial, industrial or agricultural use show only 11 out of the 30 banks estimating these at more than 20 percent of their total security loans. *Hearings Pursuant to S. Res. 71*, appendix, part 7, p. 1012.

[3] Haney, Logan and Gavens, *Brokers' Loans*, N. Y., 1932, pp. 7-8. "Our study leads to the general conclusion that brokers' loans run parallel in their movements to the movements of the stock market more than 70 percent of the time. *They tend to lag the movemens of the stock market*, however, and the divergencies between the movements of brokers' loans and the stock market nearly all occur at turning points in the stock market." (Italics the writer's.)

[4] B. H. Beckhart, *The New York Money Market*, N. Y., 1932, vol. iii, p. 123.

Source of Funds

The sources of funds going into speculative or investment channels are (1) the margin and (2) the loan. The source of funds for the loan is the main subject of this chapter.

Loans to brokers come both from banks and from individuals and business firms. Normally the majority of them come from the former source. As there are considerable differences between the lending practices of the large New York City banks and of out of town banks, most of which are correspondents of the New York City banks, these groups will be treated separately.

The New York City banks occupy a key position in the brokers' loan market.[5] The location of the principal stock exchange of the country in New York City makes immediate demands for funds felt at this point. At times when other lending agencies are desirous of making loans to brokers, they transmit funds to the large New York banks, who act as agents. Daily settlements on the Stock Exchange leave uncleared balances between brokers and it is necessary for them to borrow in order to cover their daily requirements. Sudden demands for loans, therefore, fall on the larger New York City banks. Due to the size of this market, its existence cannot be overlooked by the Federal Reserve Bank of New York.

[5] The data on brokers' loans for New York City reporting member banks have been published by the Federal Reserve Board each Friday for the close of business the previous Wednesday since January, 1926. For the period before 1926, the data are supplied by a group of daily reporting banks to the Federal Reserve Bank of New York. These data, covering the years 1917 through January, 1926, were published in the *Federal Reserve Bulletin*, 1926, pp. 780 *et seq.* Most of the daily reporting banks were also reporting member banks, but the early data are less complete, though they were only about 3 percent less in January, 1926, the only month in which both published series overlap.

Out of town banks are accustomed to keeping deposits with their New York correspondents to facilitate the clearing of checks. Fluctuation in the amount of these deposits is considerable. They act as a kind of secondary reserve for the out of town banks, being left in New York, they earn interest if no alternative investment is present. If the call loan rate is more favorable than the rate paid on deposits, they are loaned to brokers.[6] In case loans are made, the out of town banks treat their New York call loans as secondary reserves also, withdrawing them upon quick notice when they need currency for local circulation. Thus, the loans made by New York banks for out of town banks are unstable and the New York banks undertake the responsibility of replacing the sums withdrawn from the market. In other words, the New York City banks carrying accounts for out of town banks feel a dual responsibility first toward the brokers to whom they have made loans and second toward the out of town banks whose funds they have loaned.

The heading "loans for the account of others" in the reports by member banks of brokers' loans includes loans from any sources other than banks which are correspondent banks of those New York City banks which make the reports. This classification includes foreign corporations and banks, domestic corporations, individuals and estates or trust funds. There is some overlapping between these figures and the loans ostensibly made for the account of out of town banks because the latter sometimes include sums of

[6] Loans for the account of out of town banks were not reported separately before 1926, though "loans for the account of correspondents", reported before 1926, represent loans for the account of out of town banks plus loans for the account of other correspondents of New York City banks. The Banking Act of 1933 forbade the payment of interest on these deposits. The banks have, since then, complained of a mass withdrawal of out of town banks' deposits but the data do not bear out their contention.

money given them by their depositors for use in the call loan market with their own funds which are sent to New York for that purpose. While the majority of these loans are made by business corporations, private banks and some foreign banks are included in the classification " others."

The effect of a loan transaction of this type on the banking system is somewhat as follows. The lending corporation withdraws the sum of money from its bank and lends it to a broker. If the broker uses the funds thus borrowed to pay off a loan to a bank the net effect is a decrease in deposits for the banking system. The reserves required by the banking system are then correspondingly decreased. Thus loans for the account of others can be increased without limit insofar as this limitation results from the necessity imposed upon the banking system of maintaining the required reserves against deposits. But the aforementioned responsibility of the New York banks toward the brokers makes them replace any sums suddenly withdrawn from the call loan market by others. Thus loans for the account of others become a contingent liability of the banking system.

THE FEDERAL RESERVE SYSTEM AND SECURITY SPECULATION

Operations of the Reserve banks in the open money markets are conducted for the most part in New York City. The Federal Reserve Bank of New York and the Open Market Investment Committees buy in that market for the account of the eleven out of town Reserve banks. For this reason, the effects of extensive open market operations by the Reserve banks are reflected, as a rule, in the condition of large New York City banks. Since these banks are largely stock exchange institutions, it would appear to be obvious that open market purchases by the Federal Reserve System would result in additions to brokers' loans.

Loans to Brokers by New York City Banks

When the amount of loans to brokers by New York City banks is compared with the rate of interest, it is found that they do not increase with increases in interest rates. That is, New York banks do not make more brokers' loans at times when this operation is profitable. The reverse seems rather to be the case. The reason for this apparently illogical conduct is that low interest rates coincide with the presence of surplus funds, and surplus funds in New York City often have their origin in the open market operations of the Federal Reserve banks.

Chart 7 shows a comparison between brokers' loans made by New York City banks and open market holdings of the Reserve banks—both of United States securities and of bills,

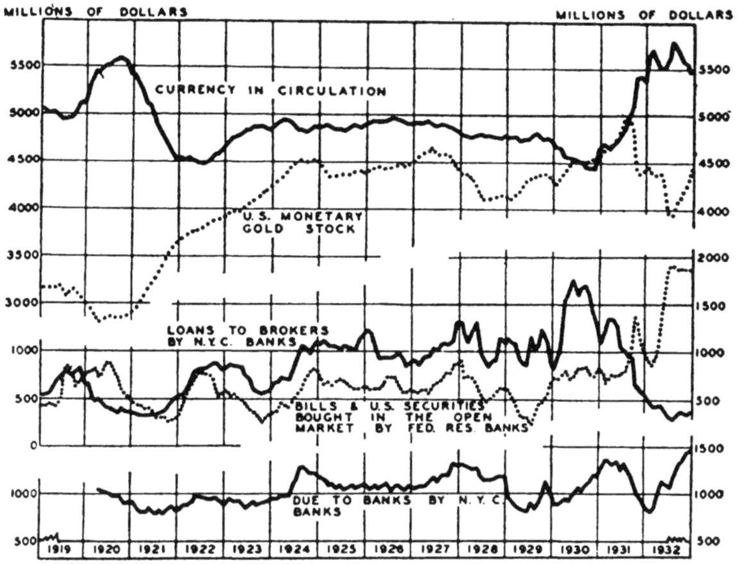

CHART 7. LOANS TO BROKERS FOR THE ACCOUNT OF NEW YORK CITY BANKS AND FACTORS CAUSING CHANGES IN THESE LOANS

Data from Federal Reserve Board

the latter corrected for seasonal variations. It is when the purchase of bills exceeds the amount required to care for the seasonal needs of the bill market that there is an excess of loanable funds in New York.

Periods when open market holdings of Reserve banks and loans to brokers by New York banks differed widely were: (1) In 1920 when the surplus credit released by the Reserve banks was used to supply the means of maintaining legal reserves behind the large amount of currency then in circulation and to provide gold for export. (2) In 1931 and 1932 when the same situation held. (3) From November, 1925, through February, 1926, when a rapid increase in the demand for credit extension by stock market operators led New York banks to increase their reserves through rediscounting. (4) During 1929 when the New York banks were forced to stabilize the brokers loan market by making sudden increases at times when corporations withdrew funds in order to make those payments which occur seasonally in the course of their businesses. The New York banks obtained funds for this purpose through rediscounting. (5) During 1930 when loans for the account of New York banks rose to very high levels whereas open market holdings of Reserve banks rose by a lesser amount, due to the added reserves obtained as a result of the declining circulation of currency and gold imports.

These facts indicate that credit extended by the Reserve banks by means of open market purchases has tended first to supply the needs of gold exports or currency use and, lacking these demands, has gone into the brokers' loan market.

Outside bankers' deposits in New York City banks have been considered to be the chief source of funds for brokers' loans by these banks. When the line at the bottom of Chart 7 is examined it will be seen that increases and decreases in these deposits do at times correspond with changes in own account brokers' loans. The necessity of paying interest on these deposits originally forced the New York banks to lend them.[7] These changes in available funds do not explain all changes in loans for own account. There are times when bankers' deposits in New York banks are large and the New York banks fear their imminent withdrawal for currency. At such times they hold large reserves against these deposits. This explains why bankers' deposits were not loaned in 1931, 1932 and the early part of 1933.

Furthermore, the gradual increase in own account brokers' loans which took place at a faster rate than the increase in open market holdings of Reserve banks between 1924 and 1929 was partly due to a process of economizing on reserves through shifts of demand deposits into the time deposit category. In the case of New York City banks in the Borough of Manhattan, such a shift would reduce the reserve requirements from 13 percent of the part of the demand deposits shifted to 3 per cent. In June, 1926, time deposits for the reporting member banks in New York City were 13.9 percent of total net deposits. In June, 1929, they were 18 per cent and in June, 1930, they were 20.2 per cent of net deposits. In June, 1932, they had once again returned to only 13.2 per cent of the total. Thus, time deposits were high at the time when brokers' loans were in demand.

The proceeds of rediscounts at the Reserve banks have less often been used in the brokers' loan market than have the proceeds of open market purchases of the System. But at times when the New York City banks must of necessity step in to stabilize the market, they may resort to rediscounting to supply the means of doing so for temporary periods. The data do not show any relationship between brokers'

[7] Miss Myers has given this interest charge a prominent place among factors causing the New York call money market to exist. *The New York Money Market*, vol. i, *Origins and Development*, N. Y., 1931, pp. 125, 269-273.

loans by any group of banks and the volume of bills which they discounted at the Reserve banks except in the case of New York City reporting member banks. During 1928 and 1929 rapid withdrawals of the funds of others were taking place periodically with equally rapid returns of the funds withdrawn in less than the fifteen days for which New York banks could obtain rediscount accommodation on their own notes. As there were no other loans held by New York banks which they could call and as they did not at that time carry excess reserves to cover the contingent liability resulting from the large volume of loans to brokers by others, they used the privilege of rediscount to tide themselves over the emergencies. The Federal Reserve Bank of New York allowed its facilities to be used to support stock speculation in 1928 and 1929. The similarity of the curve representing bills discounted by these banks and the curve representing loans to brokers by the same banks is so striking that it is shown on Chart 8.

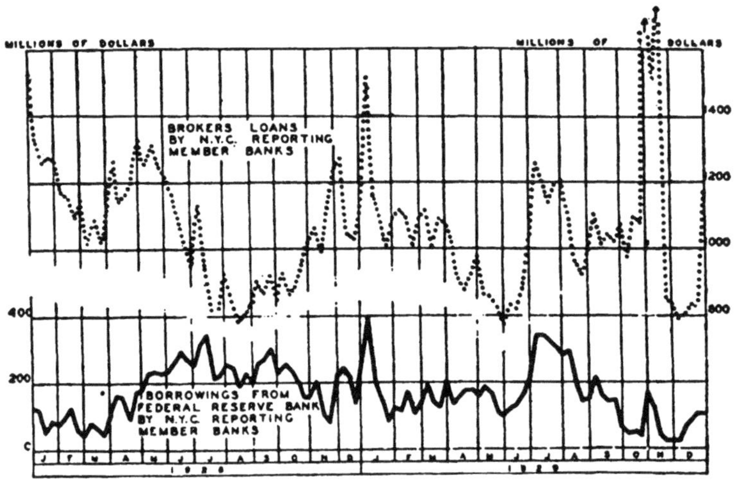

CHART 8. LOANS TO BROKERS FOR THE ACCOUNT OF NEW YORK CITY BANKS AND BORROWINGS FROM THE FEDERAL RESERVE BANK OF NEW YORK BY THESE BANKS

Data from Federal Reserve Board

Loans to Brokers for the Account of Out of Town Banks

In looking for causes of variations in loans for the account of out of town banks we shall first examine interest rates in order to determine the role of the profit motive in shaping the loan policies of banks outside New York. Differentials between interest rates on the various types of loans customarily made by outside banks explain the shifts in the relative importance of brokers' loans in their portfolios. Chart 9 shows a weighted average of the difference between

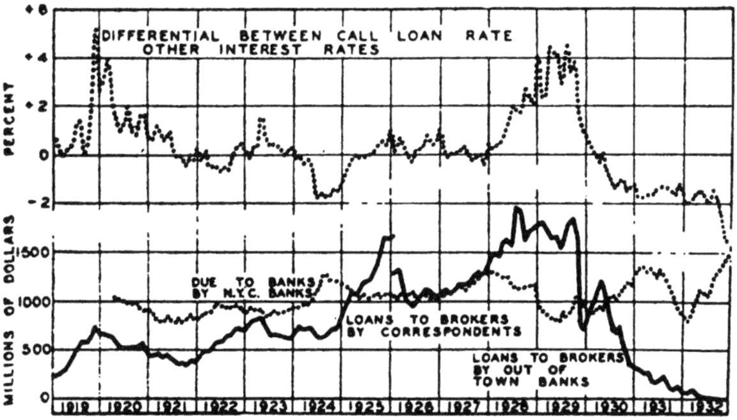

CHART 9. LOANS TO BROKERS BY OUT OF TOWN BANKS
Data on Loans to brokers since 1926 from Federal Reserve Board
Data on loans to brokers before 1926 from Federal Reserve Bank of New York
Data on interest rates computed by the author
Data on bankers' balances from Federal Reserve Board.

the call loan renewal rate and the rates on government bonds, corporate bonds and commercial paper, weighted according to their relative importance in the loan portfolios of banks outside New York. A close relationship between variations in this rate differential and loans to brokers by banks outside New York City, except during 1931 when there was a bias in the rate data due to the fact that the call loan renewal rate was an artificial rate at which no loans were being made, establishes the importance of rate considerations in inducing out of town banks to lend money at call. Consequently loans to brokers by out of town banks have varied in a direction opposite to that of loans to brokers by New York City banks.

It is apparent that a call loan rate at a level more attractive than the rate paid on other securities in which secondary reserves of banks are customarily invested induces out of town banks to lend to New York City brokers. The funds loaned are withdrawn from their deposits in New York City banks as is shown on Chart 9. The New York City banks then withdraw their own funds from the market, turning over the loans to their out of town correspondents, unless the demand for brokers' loans is so great that the funds of both sets of banks can be used. Bankers' balances held in New York serve, in this way, as a reservoir for keeping the funds of out of town banks in New York for use in the brokers' loan market over periods when rates are not high. At some times of year such funds are withdrawn completely for local use and New York banks must supply the void in the brokers' loan market with their own funds. Chart 10, showing a comparison of typical seasonal variations in loans to brokers from out of town sources and from New York

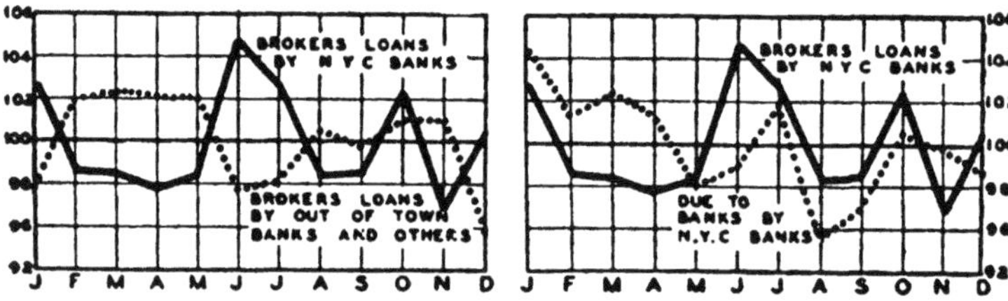

CHART 10. SEASONAL VARIATIONS IN BROKERS' LOANS
Computed by the author

banks, indicates that seasonal variations of these two types of loans are offsetting and that the chief factors causing these variations with the seasons are deposits and withdrawals of funds left on deposit in New York by out of town banks.

Loans to Brokers for the Account of Others

At the time when the amount of loans for others was first announced, they totalled 585 million dollars, while loans to brokers from all sources were 3126 million dollars. This was 18.7 per cent of the total. It was not until March, 1928, that these loans became one third of the total (1247 million dollars out of a total of 3761 million dollars.) Exactly one year later they exceeded one half of the total and remained more than that fraction until November, 1929, when a rapid drop in interest rates, following immediately upon the collapse of the stock market, led others to withdraw more than half of their funds from Wall Street. Since that date loans from this source have constantly declined. They were less than 2 per cent of the total in the spring of 1932. On November 16, 1931, the banks belonging to the New York Clearing House agreed to cease making new loans to brokers for others than banks.

Chart 11 shows a comparison of loans for the account of others with the call loan renewal rate. It is obvious that the high rate attracted these funds to this market and that when the rate declined they were rapidly withdrawn. Out of town banks also supplied funds at times when high rates ruled and withdrew them when rates fell. Consequently the liability of the New York banks arose from a double source and they leaned heavily upon their Federal Reserve bank to obtain the means of meeting this liability. The Federal Reserve Bank of New York assisted them in spite of the express prohibition of the uses of its resources for security speculation contained in section 13 of the Federal Reserve Act.

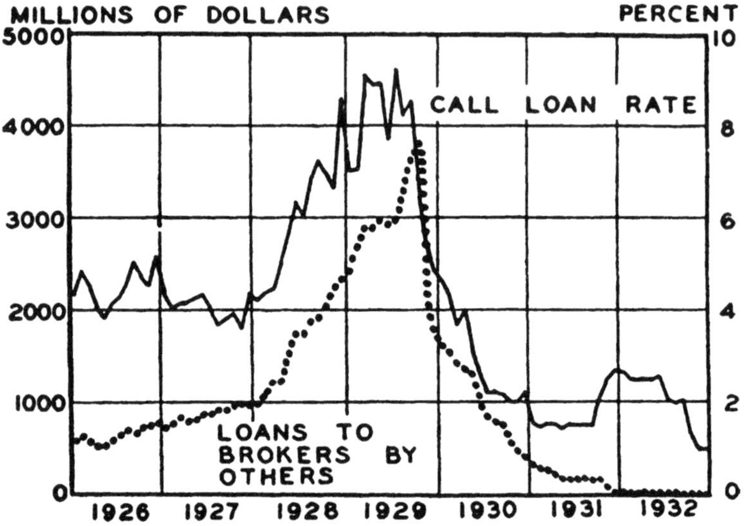

CHART 11. LOANS TO BROKERS FOR THE ACCOUNT OF "OTHERS"
Data from Federal Reserve Board

In considering call loan rates as an inducement to corporations to lend directly to brokers we are faced with the apparent contradiction between the low totals of their loans of this type in 1919 and the high totals in 1928 and 1929, although call loan rates were high in both periods. It is necessary to analyze the possible alternative uses of funds as well as their sources, to determine why this situation existed in 1928 and 1929 only. The relative attractiveness of alternative uses in 1919 and 1920 and again in 1928 and 1929 may be judged by a comparison of the yields on various types on investments in those periods. From this table it is evident that a wider differential existed between the call rate and the yields on securities which might have been bought by those lenders included under the heading "others" in 1928-1929 than in 1919-1920. Furthermore, the high yields of common stocks in 1919 and 1920 prevented the issuance of stocks for the purpose of acquiring funds to lend to brokers.

TABLE 6

YIELDS OF INVESTMENT SECURITIES DURING PERIODS OF HIGH INTEREST RATES

Date	*Call Loan Rate* (percent)	*Yields of High Grade Bonds* (percent)	*Yields of U. S. Liberty and Treasury Bonds* (percent)	*Dividend Yields of Common Stocks* (percent)	*Loans for the Account of Others* (millions of dollars)
1919 March ...	5.05	5.18	4.77	7.30	
June	6.30	5.17	4.74	6.62	
Sept.	5.62	5.32	4.78	6.51	
Dec.	8.06	5.48	4.96	6.48	
1920 March ...	8.13	5.65	5.14	6.87	
June	7.47	6.10	5.59	7.54	
Sept.	7.07	5.95	5.63	7.80	
Dec.	7.00	6.03	5.76	8.53	
1928 March ...	4.47	4.37	3.30	4.14	1,247
June	6.32	4.50	3.40	4.12	1,736
Sept.	7.26	4.57	3.54	3.72	1,924
Dec.	8.60	4.59	3.53	3.56	2,319
1929 March ...	9.10	4.69	3.76	3.28	2,879
June	7.70	4.73	3.71	3.51	2,940
Sept.	8.50	4.76	3.70	3.19	3,642
Dec.	4.83	4.63	3.46	4.83	1,790

Sources of data on bond yields: Standard Statistics Co.'s average of yields of 60 high grade bonds.

Sources of data on stock yields: Standard Statistics Co.'s average of yields of 33 dividend paying industrials, 1919-1920, and of 50 industrials, 1928-1929.

Loans for the account of others came, for the most part, from non-banking sources. The share of business corporations in supplying money for this purpose, as reported by six large New York City banks to the sub-committee of the

Committee on Banking and Currency of the United States Senate as of September 17, 1929, was 58 per cent of the total.[8] The share of individuals was 18 per cent, of investment trusts 8 per cent and of foreign lenders 9.5 per cent. From this information Professor Beckhart estimated the share of corporations on that date as 2,021 million dollars.[9]

There was less inducement to lend in the call loan market in 1919 and 1920. There were also less surplus funds in the hands of corporations. Post-war conditions resulted in a need for new plants and the adaptation of old plants to peacetime needs. The boom and period of high interest rates in 1928 and 1929 came at the end of a long period of relatively great prosperity and stability. It found the corporations in possession of surplus funds which they had never before had.

Loans to Bank Depositors on Securities and Brokers' Loans

As previously stated, loans to bank depositors on security collateral provide one means of supplying the funds for carrying on operations in securities with other people's money. These loans rose at a slower rate than did loans to brokers although they rose sharply at a few times, being liquidated slowly, if at all, after each rise.

Chart 12 shows a comparison between an estimate of loans to customers on securities by reporting member banks and brokers' loans for the years, 1920 to 1932.[10] It is obvious,

[8] *Hearings Pursuant to S. Res. 71*, appendix, part 7, p. 1024.

[9] B. H. Beckhart, *The New York Money Market*, N. Y., 1932, vol. iii, p. 168.

[10] The figures on which this chart is based were obtained from Professor Beckhart, to whom the author wishes to express acknowledgment. They were computed as follows:

(1) Loans to customers on securities for New York City reporting member banks after 1926 were obtained by subtracting the loans to

from an examination of the chart, that the major increases in customers' loans on securities came at times of liquidation

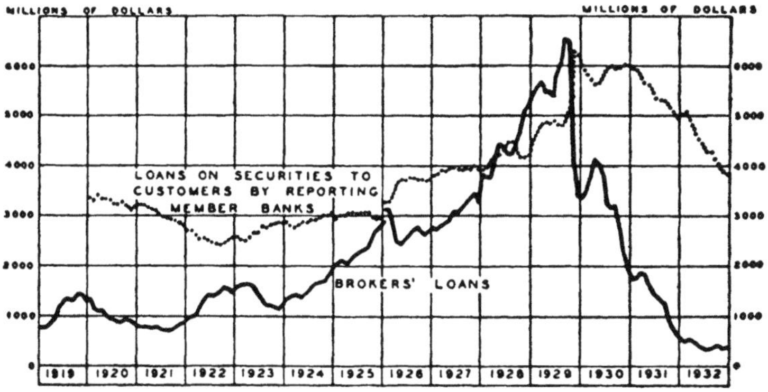

CHART 12. LOANS TO BANK DEPOSITORS ON SECURITY COLLATERAL

Data computed by Professor B. Haggott Beckhart from data supplied by Federal Reserve Board

of brokers' loans—1923, 1926, 1929 and 1930—and that these loans in turn were not ever decreased as rapidly as

brokers by these banks from their total security loans. This part of the data is accurate.

(2) Loans to customers on securities for New York City banks before 1926 was obtained by subtracting from total security loans for reporting member banks the loans to brokers by those banks which reported to the Federal Reserve Bank of New York. Since the banks in these two groups were not identical, this figure is an estimate. Its accuracy is enhanced by the fact that the two series for brokers' loans were approximately the same during January, 1926.

(3) Loans to customers on securities for out of town banks was obtained by subtracting from total security loans for out of town reporting member banks the loans to brokers by out of town banks after 1926 and by correspondents before that date.

(4) Loans to customers on securities by reporting member banks are obtained by adding the estimate made for New York banks and correcting for seasonal variations.

There is a bias in the data due to the method of estimation which probably conceals the true extent of the rise in security loans to customers before 1926.

were loans to brokers. These observations lead us inevitably to the conclusion that a large part of the loans to bank depositors on securities originated in the taking over by banks of liabilities of their depositors previously contracted to brokers. If such is the case, the advantage to banks of loans to brokers, that they are easily liquidated, disappears, except in isolated cases of banks whose loans to brokers were taken over by other banks.

The shift of brokers' loans into customers' loans on securities introduces a cumulative element into the brokers' loan market. Brokers' loans have been readily increased at times of open market purchases by the Reserve banks. Whenever the Reserve banks have sold securities, out of town banks and others have taken over the brokers' loans which had previously been made by New York City banks. During periods of liquidation, when no banks wished to leave their loans to brokers outstanding, they trusted their own depositors sufficiently to take over their liabilities to brokers. The result of this shifting process has been that a considerable amount of security credit has been left over after each deflation. This credit always awaits an opportunity to be shifted to other lenders. If other factors induce out of town banks and others to increase their loans to brokers before these customer loans on securities are liquidated by means of the withdrawal of purchasing power from the markets for goods, the credit remains outstanding until the next period when the Reserve banks supply funds to the New York banks by means of open market operations.

The indirect relationship between open market operations by the Reserve bank and the brokers' loan market has already been established. When Reserve bank credit is not needed to supply the means of converting deposits into currency or of making gold payments abroad or to prepare for such emergencies, as was the case in 1932, the brokers' loan market stands ready to absorb surplus funds of the money market. When it has once absorbed this surplus, it retains the funds previously absorbed, even though they may later on be needed for other purposes. Even though banks liquidate their loans to brokers they are forced to lend substantial amounts to their depositors on security collateral, in order to enable them to continue to meet their commitments. The slowness with which the final liquidation of loans to depositors on securities takes place, when no shift back into the brokers' loan market is possible, makes these loans a potential source of danger to the stability of banks. Thus loans for the purpose of carrying securities are essentially illiquid. They cannot be realized upon at quick notice except from the proceeds of loans by other banks.

Opinions of Federal Reserve Authorities on the Brokers' Loan Market

That the Reserve banks realized that the proceeds of some of their rediscounts were used to increase loans to brokers is shown by their answers to the questionnaire sent by the subcommittee of the Senate Banking and Currency Committee in 1930. In reply to the question relative to the more important considerations leading to changes in rates of rediscount since January, 1924, among other reasons given for rate increases were the growth in speculation and the use of local funds in the brokers' loan market. All Reserve banks agreed that the reason for the increases in rates during 1928 and 1929 was to check speculation. The same factor influenced only two Reserve banks in their rate increases in 1925.

The Federal Reserve banks, in the same document as that quoted above, gave voice to the fact that they recognized that open market purchases of government securities by the System stimulated the growth of brokers' loans. A digest of replies to the question relative to the principal reasons for, and main consequences of, each of the major operations in government securities since January, 1922, indicates that the Reserve banks considered an increase in brokers' loans to have been the result of each major purchase except that of October, 1929, through December, 1930. Reduction in brokers' loans did not follow most of the sales operations.[11]

The Federal Reserve System has come more and more in recent years to follow the state of the security loan markets in shaping its broader credit policies. It has already been mentioned that only two Reserve banks considered the state of the market for brokers' loans in determining their rate policies during 1925. In 1927 one Reserve bank objected to the rate reductions ordered by the Board on account of the growth of speculation taking place at that time[12] while one other Reserve bank—Boston—feared the possible consequences of such a policy on speculative activity but did not raise any objection. In 1928 and 1929, Federal Reserve policy was directed entirely toward restraining the expansion of brokers' loans.

But Federal Reserve policies dictated with a view to reducing the total volume of loans to brokers were circumvented by the actions of lenders other than banks. That these loans—referred to by many as " bootleg " loans—were a grave source of danger to the stability of the credit system and were the chief cause of the continuation of stock market activity after the Federal Reserve System had instituted measures for strict control was the universal opinion of witnesses testifying on the operations of the National and Federal Reserve Banking Systems before the Senate Committee on Banking and Currency in 1931. Mr. Charles Mitchell, at that time Chairman of the National City Bank, stated, " Loans for others were a great contributing factor to the

[11] *Hearings Pursuant to S. Res. 71*, appendix, part 6, pp. 795-796.

[12] See chap. ii, p. 28.

inflation that took place in the security market." This opinion was concurred in by Mr. J. H. Case, Governor Harrison of the Federal Reserve Bank of New York, Mr. A. C. Miller, member of the Federal Reserve Board, and Mr. Owen D. Young. Governor Harrison was of the opinion that attempts to control speculation, inasmuch as they resulted in increases in the call loan rate, had the effect of increasing the funds available to speculators, instead of decreasing them. This result was due to the potent effect of the rate of interest on the supplies of credit obtainable from bootleg sources.[13]

The seepage of Federal Reserve credit into the brokers' loan market is contrary to the purpose of the Federal Reserve Act as interpreted by the Board in its *Annual Report* for 1923, in which it stated that the resources of the System should not be put to speculative uses. In the Banking Act of 1933, there are provisions for preventing the proceeds of rediscount advances from being so used. It is through open market operations that the Reserve banks have, in the past, supplied funds for speculation in securities. Not only have no safeguards been set up against a recurrence of this misuse of Federal Reserve credit but the government of the United States, which has complete charge of shaping Federal Reserve policy at the time of writing, is definitely committed to the theory that such open market purchases of securities are a method of releasing credit for business purposes.[14]

SUMMARY

The relationship of Federal Reserve policy, particularly the open market policy of the Federal Reserve System, to

[13] *Hearings Pursuant to S. Res. 71*, part 1.

[14] The Reserve banks are at present under the obligation to purchase $3,000,000,000 worth of securities when the President of the United States shall see fit that they do so.

brokers' loans has been shown to be a close one. The supply of credit available to the market has been a factor influencing speculative activity at times when the money market has not been suffering from external or internal drains due to gold exports or to currency hoarding. These supplies of fresh credit have been obtained through the great open market purchases by the Reserve banks. Corresponding open market sales have not had a counterbalancing restrictive effect upon speculative activity due to the ease with which speculators have been able to shift their loans from loans by brokers to loans by banks. Thus Federal Reserve open market policies, particularly purchases of United States Government securities, contributed greatly to over-speculation in securities and should, in the future, be undertaken on a smaller scale.

Supply factors have been shown to be important in determining the amount of brokers' loans made by New York City banks. Since money is plentiful at times when rates are low, we may expect this part of brokers' loans to increase at these times. This relationship between brokers' loans and interest rates does not indicate cause and effect, since borrowing by brokers is not stimulated by a low call loan rate. If this were so, high rates would check the growth of brokers' loans which they did not succeed in doing during 1928 and 1929. Both are probably common results of the same cause—an excess of available surplus funds in an earlier period. Once speculative activity has been initiated and encouraged, demand becomes the determining factor in the amount loaned to brokers. An increase in demand, originally stimulated by increased money lent by New York City banks, causes rates to rise and attracts the funds of other lenders, both banks and others.

The Federal Reserve System has come to regard the state of the brokers' loan market as a guide to its broader credit policies. In earlier years a few Reserve banks took cognizance of such lending by commercial banks when setting their rates. In 1928 and 1929 the entire policy of the Federal Reserve System was directed toward limiting the volume of loans to brokers. Due to the inability of the Reserve banks to deal in paper arising out of such transactions, the System has relied upon indirect control through the rate of interest to control the brokers' loan market. Further study of the efficacy of indirect control will be the subject of the next two chapters.

CHAPTER VII

FEDERAL RESERVE POLICY AND RATES OF INTEREST

CONTROL OF CREDIT THROUGH THE RATE OF INTEREST

THE last three chapters have dealt with the direct effects of Federal Reserve policy upon various kinds of loans. Through the eligibility requirements of the System an attempt has been made to improve and standardize commercial lending methods. The fact that member banks can obtain accommodation as readily, if not more readily, on their government bonds as on eligible paper has prevented the eligibility requirements of the Federal Reserve System from having any effect upon the lending policies of member banks. In its effort to support the bankers' acceptance market with a view to establishing a large and flourishing market, the System has only prevented the establishment of an outside market. But later on, when the Reserve banks stopped buying acceptances in large volume, a small independent market developed in New York City. No outside market has succeeded in maintaining a permanent foothold. In aiming to influence directly the volume of credit extended by other lending agencies through open market operations, the System has succeeded only in bringing about great increases in the extension of credit for speculation in securities—a type of credit which resists all efforts at liquidation.

Efforts of the System have been directed more and more toward influencing the volume of loans not directly under its control through shaping its credit policies with a view to influencing rates of interest in the money and capital markets.

Open market operations have been engaged in to prepare for later changes in discount rates. It was hoped that, by this means, the volume of credit in use would adjust itself to changes in rates.

The use of Federal Reserve operations to influence the volume of credit recognized by lending agencies presupposes two intermediate relationships. The first is the relationship between Federal Reserve operations and rates of interest in all markets where business firms borrow. The second is the relationship between rates of interest ruling in those markets and the volume of loans made in them. An answer to the question as to whether these relationships hold will tell us whether Federal Reserve operations directed toward altering rates of interest will alter business borrowing and to what extent that is so. The first of these relationships, the relationship between Federal Reserve operations and rates of interest in the money and capital markets will be the subject of this chapter. The second relationship will occupy Chapter VIII.

Interest Rate Differentials

In determining which rates of interest to use as samples of rates ruling in the money and capital markets, the following were chosen for the reasons given:

(1) The rate on prime commercial paper with four to six months' maturity. This rate is published daily in the newspapers and monthly averages of daily rates are obtainable. While not representing a large market, this is a market which is relatively free from control.

(2) The open market rate on prime bankers' acceptances of 90 days' maturity at New York City. This is the maximum maturity allowed for rediscount at Federal Reserve banks and, except in the case of import or export credits and agricultural paper, is the maximum allowed for purchase.

(3) The call loan renewal rate, which is the rate applying to all loans made on the New York Stock Echange which are not new loans, and, therefore, applies to the majority of loans in existence. It is unfortunate that this rate is at times an artificial rate, as the Stock Exchange frequently "pegs" the rate, driving borrowers or lenders to entering into their transactions outside the Exchange.

(4) For customers' loans at banks, the minimum rates ruling on prime commercial loans of less than 90 days' maturity. These are reported to the Federal Reserve Board from banks in a selected group of cities in which Federal Reserve banks or branches of Federal Reserve banks are located. The data do not represent true minimum rates but the minimum of rates applying to the bulk of the loans made. It is evident to anyone examining the original data that they are subject to some errors.

(5) The average yield of United States Treasury notes and certificates of indebtedness, as published by the Federal Reserve Board.

(6) The yields of various classes of high grade bonds published by the Standard Statistics Co.

(7) The yields of preferred stocks published by the Standard Statistics Co.

(8) The yields of common stocks published by the Standard Statistics Co. For the period, 1919 through 1928, this represents the yield of 33 dividend paying industrial common stocks. For 1926 through 1932, the series has been computed for 50 dividend paying common stocks.[1] For the three overlapping years, 1926 through 1928, the two series move in unison though their levels differ.

(9) The yield of United States Liberty and Treasury bonds, as published by the Federal Reserve Board.

[1] This series was discontinued in the last quarter of 1932.

(10) The yield of urban real estate bonds published by the United States Department of Commerce in the *Survey of Current Business*. These data represent only a few issues, those that were floated during the month in question by a limited number of investment bankers, and are therefore inaccurate. They are the only data obtainable on rates in the urban real estate mortgage market, however.

Comparison of Rates Ruling in the Money and Capital Markets

Chart 13 shows a comparison between one example of a rate in the money market, one of a rate in the bond market

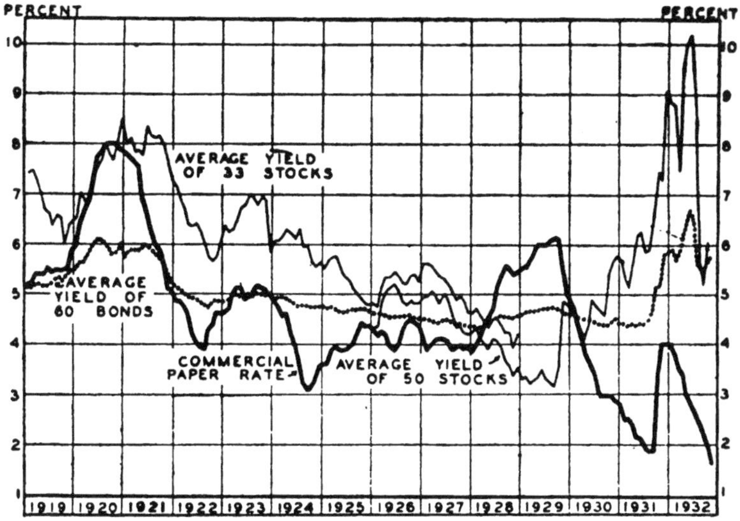

CHART 13. INTEREST RATES IN THREE TYPICAL MARKETS
Data from Standard Statistics Co.

and the yield of common stocks. This chart shows that rates ruling in all markets have the same cyclical variations, though varying amplitudes of variation, for the years, 1919 through 1923. The rate on commercial paper moved before the others. This was followed by yields of long term bonds. Yields of common stocks moved somewhat after yields of bonds.

After 1923 a new situation developed. Bond yields ceased following the commercial paper rate in their minor cyclical movements although they did rise, but to a slight extent, in 1928 and 1929, when the commercial paper rate rose very steeply. The yields of stocks showed both major and minor cylical variations which were opposite in direction to the cycles in the commercial paper rate. After the middle of 1931, bond yields rose with yields of stocks. Commercial paper rates showed a corresponding rise, which was reversed within two months, although bond yields and the yields of common stock remained high.

Evidently factors affecting the rate of interest on short term funds are transmitted to yields on long term loans and common stocks only at times when conditions are favorable to such a relationship. At other times, changes in underlying conditions bringing about changes in the short term rates of interest, such as the action of the Federal Reserve Banks, have no effects outside the short term markets and so cannot influence the rate of interest which business pays for funds in the long term markets.

There is a close correspondence between rates of interest in short term markets. The exceptions are the call loan rate which moves in cycles of greater amplitude than other short term rates and the rates charged customers at banks which show resistance to change.

Rates of interest in the capital markets, on the other hand, show some correspondence, although there has been a steady decline in the yield of long term government bonds relative to other bond yields since the close of the World War. The yields of preferred stocks correspond, in their movements, to the yields of corporate bonds. But, as pointed out above, the yields of common stocks show independent movements between 1924 and the middle of 1931.

The data shown on Chart 13 indicate that rate differentials are as typical of economic activity as are rate similarities. These disparities, except in the period preceding 1924, are not simply uniform differences due to risk factors, nor are they differences set up by the fact that changes in rates in one market are transmitted to rates in other markets at a later time. They are so lacking in uniformity that rates of interest in various markets may undergo independent cyclical variations. These inequalities are rather between broad groups of markets—the short term markets, the long term markets for fixed interest obligations and the market for common stocks—than between individual markets. The extent to which theoretical studies of the problem of interest have allowed for these differentials must, therefore, be examined.

Theoretical Basis for Rate Differentials

Professor Fisher, in his admirable work, *The Theory of Interest*,[2] defines interest as measuring the rate of exchange between present goods and future goods. Factors determining the discount given for goods available immediately are " impatience " (or " time preference "), " investment opportunity " and " uncertainty " (or " risk.") Time preference, the subjective factor, is the cause limiting the supply of funds available for investment.

The objective factor determining the direction of investment of those savings is the principle of investment opportunity. Among the several uses to which savings may be applied that one rendering the maximum present value is chosen. But the present value of an investment yielding future income is regulated by the rate of interest at which

[2] Irving Fisher, *The Theory of Interest*, N. Y., 1930.

future income items are discounted to find their present worth. Therefore, that one of the investment opportunities is selected which will yield the maximum present value in terms of the current rate of interest. When current rates of interest are low investments yielding a high future income but a low immediate income are preferred.

The added principle of uncertainty or risk—Fisher's third variable—makes investors prefer to use their savings in that form of investment which they think will give them a high future return at times when current interest rates are low. It also divides investors into two classes—those willing to take risks and those who wish to avoid them. This division makes for the existence of a persistent disparity between rates of interest on safe investments and on less safe investments. This disparity is widened at times of imminent social unrest.

Professor Fisher's theory depends upon the equilibrium principle that " a low rate of interest favors the choice of the more ascending income streams, but also that the choice of such income streams reacts to raise the rate of interest." [8] By this action rates of interest in different markets should be equalized except for the disparity due to varying degrees of risk and varying desires of investors for safe or risky investments. They should show the same direction of change, though varying degrees of change. Furthermore, the yields of risky investments should always be higher than the yields of safe investments, which has not always been the case. Professor Fisher omits from his analysis the effects of time adjustment on the direction of interest rates and the effects of public misjudgments of the extent of the risk element in various investments. If the reaction brought about by the

[8] Fisher, *op. cit.*, p. 202.

choice of ascending income streams to raise rates of interest is not automatically brought into being, but is somewhat delayed, interest rate differentials may persist for long enough periods of time to cause serious economic maladjustments. Any public misjudgment of the degree of risk in a given type of investment may also unduly raise or depress rates of interest on investments of that type, without affecting the rate of interest at which the present value of future income is determined.

Professor Fisher's analysis of factors making for various preferences for investments yielding immediate and future returns and for investments with changing degrees of risk may be applied to the rate differentials which have existed in the money and capital markets since the year, 1924. The period from 1920 to 1924 was characterized by gold imports into the United States of greater magnitude than have occurred before or since that date. The addition to the gold stock brought about a condition of ease in the money and capital markets which was felt between 1922 and 1924, causing investors to seek outlets for their funds which would give them a future rather than an immediate return. This explanation may account for the fact that investments in common stocks began to be popular at that time. Since the first buyers of these stocks were able to get high immediate returns by selling out at a profit, a misjudgment of the risk element caused investors to prefer this form of investment in later years because rates of interest were then high and they believed that they were obtaining a high present return by means of buying and then reselling at a profit.

When the process of buying and selling securities to obtain a return had reached an inevitable, though somewhat belated, end, the growing feeling of uncertainty caused people to prefer safe investments, whatever the yield. Professor Fisher's theory accounts for the fact that yields on corporate long term securities, both bonds and stocks, moved rapidly upwards in 1930, 1931 and 1932 although interest rates in the short term markets and yields of United States Government bonds were declining. The prevailing feeling of uncertainty on the part of investors prevented the efforts of the Federal Reserve System at lowering interest rates from having any effect beyond a very limited market.

Thus it may be seen that the principles laid down by Professor Fisher account for many of the differentials between rates of interest ruling in different markets at the same time since 1924. But there remain other differentials to be explained—ones which result from artificial influences acting from the supply side. Since the fund of money awaiting investment arises from the savings of the people, but may be augmented by the creation of bank credit, its size at any time is somewhat under the control of the banking system. While the actions of banks and of central banks cannot increase the amount of real income in the community, these institutions can change the distribution of income by the choice which they exercise over whose credit they will recognize. Changes in the distribution of income in one period have an effect upon savings in the next period, for the process of saving is somewhat automatic. It is the result of the possession of excess income above the needs of consumption. If the banks recognize the credit of those who normally save, they artificially augment the fund available for investment in long term assets. In the period of time which we are considering, banks increased their advances through the medium of security loans, thus increasing the demand for investment by those who valued future income above present income and were, therefore, willing to purchase shares of stock even though their yield was low.

FEDERAL RESERVE OPERATIONS AS CAUSES OF CHANGING INTEREST RATES

That the operations of the Reserve banks were more frequently dictated with a view either to altering market rates of interest or to controlling speculation than for any one other cause has been brought out in Chapter II.[4] The former guide refers to short term interest rates and the latter to rates ruling on the capital markets.

The Federal Reserve Banks and Short-term Interest Rates

Short term interest rates are of two distinct types; open market interest rates, or rates ruling on paper which is discounted by some holder other than the one with whom the borrower originally negotiated the loan, and rates ruling at banks on paper which is held by them until maturity. The former, open market interest rates, always exhibit changes before the latter, customer rates.

Among the factors which the Reserve banks consider sufficiently potent to influence interest rates are (1) the discount rate and (2) open market holdings of government securities and of bankers' acceptances. The discount rate as an influence causing changes in open market interest rates was eliminated by Riefler, who observed that discount rates have always been changed after open market interest rates have changed.[5] With this conclusion we cannot quarrel because Riefler's charts offer final evidence for his conclusion. Riefler found that the volume of bills discounted influences interest rates.

The Federal Reserve banks also attempt to influence the money market through open market operations. Originally engaged in to provide Reserve banks with earning assets, to

[4] Chap. ii, pp. 29 and 37.

[5] Winfield W. Riefler, *Money Rates and Money Markets in the United States*, N. Y., 1930, p. 24.

stabilize certain parts of the money market or to influence the money market temporarily pending a change in the discount rate, these operations have come more and more to occupy an independent position among the tools of credit control. The Federal Reserve banks have claimed that they are effective and that a decline in interest rates has always followed purchases of government bonds.[6] Such a consequence logically follows a release of funds at the chief financial center or the country—New York City. But if Federal funds are in great demand to obtain Federal Reserve notes for internal circulation or to obtain gold from the Reserve banks for export, the Reserve banks may engage in open market operations without any marked influence on interest rates.

The interest rates first affected will be the rates on the securities purchased—United States securities and bankers' acceptances—and the rate on Federal funds. It is only when the banks from which securities have been purchased replace their purchases with other paper or when other banks purchase the excess Reserve balances from them in the market for Federal funds that other interest rates feel the effect of a purchase of government securities or of acceptances by the Reserve banks.

If member banks do not wish to expand their loan and investment portfolios, but fear future withdrawals of gold or of currency, they will hold these reserves as excess reserves. Smaller member banks will redeposit them in larger banks and bankers' balances will rise. These bankers' balances, being a sort of emergency reserve of banks all over the country, should not be loaned, but be held pending the emergency.

[6] *Hearings Pursuant to S. Res. 71*, appendix, part 6, pp. 795-796.

Chart 14, showing a comparison between open market holdings of securities and of bankers' acceptances, the latter corrected for seasonal variations, held by Reserve banks and open market interest rates on short term government securities and on bankers' acceptances, indicates the exceptions to the rule that open market operations influence interest rates occurred at times when gold or currency was in demand. Open market holdings of bills and securities by Reserve banks are only one of several factors influencing open market interest rates.

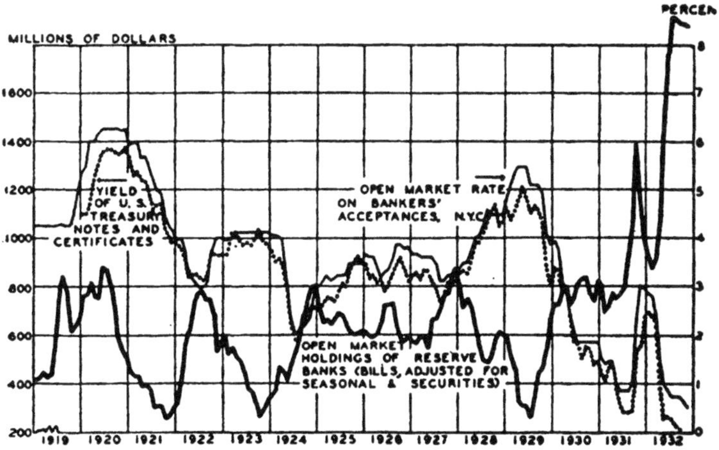

CHART 14. OPEN MARKET OPERATIONS OF FEDERAL RESERVE BANKS AND INTEREST RATES

Data on open market operations from Federal Reserve Board
Data on interest rates from Standard Statistics Co.

The rates which banks' customers pay for loans made directly at their banks show a more stable tendency than do rates of interest ruling in open markets. In some localities they change frequently, exhibiting all the characteristics of open market interest rates, though always moving after them. In other localities they reflect only the major movements of interest rates.

Customer loans at banks fall into several classifications. First, there is the classification by type of security which is shown in the data on rates supplied by the Federal Reserve Board. That this classification is without significance is evident from the fact that rates on all types of loans in the same cities show approximately the same number of changes, whereas the variation from city to city was considerable.

Another classification is according to the location of the bank. It has been frequently emphasized that banks in country places never change their lending rates whereas banks in financial centers follow rates ruling in the open money markets in making loans. A comparison of lending rates at banks with rediscount rates at Reserve banks may be made in cities where Reserve banks are located. This comparison shows that whenever the Reserve bank is located in a large center, customer rates at banks have changed before changes were made in the Reserve bank rate. But in Kansas City, a comparatively small place, customer rates did not show turning points until after the discount rate had been changed. While the data do not eliminate the possibility that discount rates are taken account of in fixing customer rates in small places, there is a strong presupposition that this is not the case. In no large financial center has this relationship held. It seems more likely that banks fix their customer rates according to the law of supply and demand, at the same time paying whatever rate of discount the local Reserve bank chooses to charge. In country places the demand for loans does not slacken when rates have been kept higher than in other places because the customers of country banks usually have no other market in which to apply for loans. The supply of funds is not cut off by an increase in the discount rate of the Reserve bank, for member banks actually increase their discounts at Reserve banks at times when rates are high, reducing them when rates are low.

The third and most significant classification of customer loans depends upon the type of customer applying for the loan. Some Reserve banks have noticed differences in rates charged to customers who can obtain accommodation from more than one bank and ones who must go to one bank only. Most of them overlooked this distinction due to the great differences shown according to geographical location of the bank. But large depositors are generally located in large cities, while country banks' depositors are usually of the small category. Furthermore, data on rates are not supplied for large and small loans. If such were the case, it is probable that we should find stability to be the rule for the small loan and sensitivity to market factors for the large loan.

There is no evidence that the discount rate charged by the Reserve bank has any influence at all upon the rate charged to the small borrower, as his rate is stable, both at times of tight and of easy credit. Rates charged to large customers vary with conditions in the open money markets, for a number of them may resort to open markets for advances if their banks charge them high rates. All of them may go to more than one bank for accommodation.

The Reserve banks exert their pressure on the money markets through changes in their holdings of United States Government securities and of bills eligible for purchase. Purchases and sales of these bills and securities influence the amount of funds available to the country for several purposes. Funds released by open market operations may be used to replace cash withdrawals from banks by the public, for gold withdrawals for export or to increase the lending power of banks. The former two uses take precedence. It the demand for funds for these two purposes is quiescent, the banks will attempt to dispose of their surplus funds, first by bidding for the available supplies of open market paper of the various kinds, and then by lowering the rates which they charge on loans to customers as an inducement to borrow. Rates of interest ruling in the money markets show approximately the same variations as are shown in the volume of rediscounts at Reserve banks. This similarity is due to the fact that both are the results of common causes —causes which influence the supply of loanable funds.

The Reserve Banks and the Yields of Government Bonds

The yields of United States Government bonds declined faster than did the yields of other investment securities after 1923. The high level of government bond yields before 1924, actually exceeding the yields of high grade municipal bonds at the time, was not due to the fact that the United States of America was considered to be a more risky venture than some of the municipalities within it, but to Federal Reserve policy.

The close of the war found a large part of the outstanding debt of the United States Government pledged to banks, which had, in turn, pledged it to the Reserve banks in order to enable the public to invest in Liberty bonds which it could not pay for. At the close of the war, the question was faced by each Reserve bank: should it free itself of the loans of this type through forced liquidation or should it support the market for government bonds? The Federal Reserve Agents reported to the Federal Reserve Board at the end of 1918 that it was advisable for the banks to expel the government bonds from their portfolios and to force permanent investors to take them over. This policy was delayed until the end of 1919 due to the aid given by the Reserve banks in the flotation of the Victory Loan in the spring of that year, a process which lasted until December. Even during the intervening period, yields of government bonds were high due to the fact that the Treasury made every effort to sell them to ultimate investors. By May, 1920, the liquidation process had gone so far that the Federal Advisory Council made the following recommendation:[7]

From a survey of present rates in force by the Federal Reserve Banks it would seem that 6 per cent is now being charged on paper secured by Liberty bonds and Victory notes. In the judgment of the council, when and if any further revision of rates should be made, there should be shown due consideration for the original subscriber of Government securities.

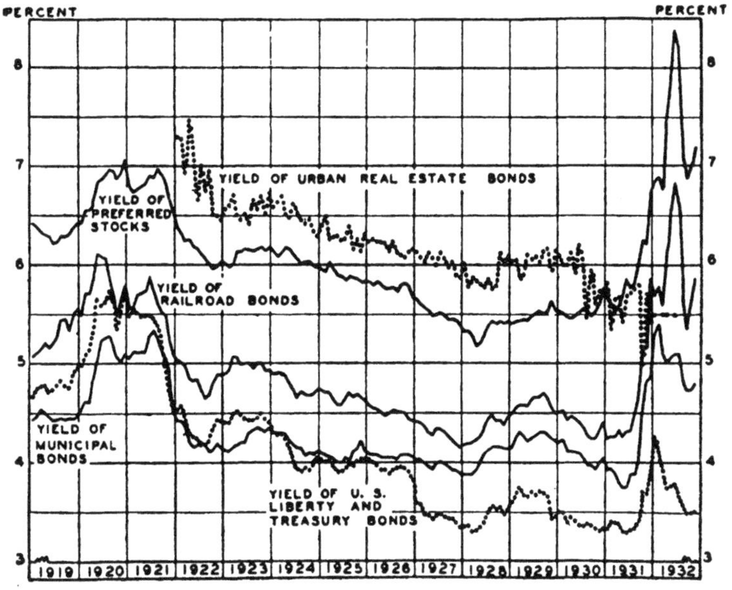

CHART 15. YIELDS OF LONG TERM SECURITIES
Data on Yields of Real Estate Bonds from *Survey of Current Business*
Other data from Standard Statistics Co.

Due consideration was not shown for the original subscriber of government securities and their price was allowed to seek

[7] Federal Reserve Board, *Annual Report*, 1920, p. 603.

its natural level until 1922, when the first major purchase of government securities by the Reserve banks took place.

The purchases of government securities by the Reserve banks of 1922, 1924 and 1927 are clearly reflected on Chart 15 in sharp declines in the yield of government bonds. The sales of securities by Reserve banks following these purchases are not reflected in corresponding rises in their yield because they were purchased at those times, not by investors, but by member banks, which were willing to make the purchases at a low yield in order to hold government bonds which they might pledge for 15-day loans at their Reserve banks. Therefore, the combined policies of the Reserve banks, first buying government securities outright and then making advances to their member banks on the basis of such security collateral, forced the yield of government bonds to lower and lower levels. There was some rise during 1928 and 1929 when investors were liquidating their holdings in order to purchase common stocks and again in the fall of 1931, when banks threw their holdings on the market in order to realize upon them to provide the means for currency withdrawals by their depositors or gold exports. Both of these situations were rectified by purchases made by the Reserve banks in 1930 and again in 1932. This analysis shows the prominence of the part played by the Federal Reserve System—both the Reserve banks and the member banks—in the determination of yields of government bonds.

The Reserve Banks and the Yields of Corporate Securities

Yields of investment securities other than government bonds have followed the latter only in their major movements. The position of the Federal Reserve System is less well defined in the determination of the yields of such securities. It is not permissible for the Reserve banks to purchase them on their own account and member banks cannot borrow at their Reserve banks on such security. The System can only influence the yields of corporate bonds if it forces outside investors or banks to replace the government bonds purchased from them by other bonds or, in the reverse case, if it induces them to purchase government securities from the proceeds of sales of corporate securities.

Since banks are large purchasers of corporate bonds, their activities in bond markets are significant factors affecting the yields of bonds. The great growth in investment holdings of banks is shown on Table 10 in Chapter IX.

The investment portfolios of banks increased steadily since the close of the World War, with the exception of the years, 1920, 1921, 1929, 1930 and 1932. These were years in which the yields of long term securities were high, as shown on Chart 15.

Variations in corporate bond yields, particularly the slow decline beginning in 1923 and continuing until 1927, may be explained by changes in the holdings of bonds by banks. The small rise in bond yields in 1928 and 1929 resulted, not from Federal Reserve policy, but from sales by investors who were transferring their holdings to common stocks. Federal Reserve policy could not have been responsible directly for this move; for the Reserve banks do not deal in the bond markets, other than the market for government bonds. Therefore, it is not clear that Federal Reserve operations cause variations in the yields of investment securities, other than the securities in which they themselves deal.

Rates ruling in the capital markets varied in the same manner as rates ruling in the money markets between the beginning of 1919 and the middle of 1924. The shortage of capital immediately following the close of the war was so intense that the resultant bidding for funds caused withdrawals from all markets. When liquidation took place, it was orderly and caused rate reductions for all kinds of securities. After the middle of 1924 bond yields declined steadily as investors accumulated funds out of savings and increased their bond holdings or left larger balances on deposit in banks, enabling the banks to increase their investment portfolios. Fluctuations in the demand for common stocks were brought about by changing investment choices of lenders and caused yields on stocks to fluctuate in a direction opposite to that of short term interest rates. When prices of common stocks rose so quickly that investors and banks sold their bond holdings in order to increase their purchases of common stocks, bond yields commenced to advance. After stock prices were liquidated in 1929 a new investment demand for bonds appeared and bond yields declined with other short term interest rates. As the depression in business deepened and showed no signs of being temporary in nature, an increasing realization on the part of investors of the inherently risky nature of bond purchases caused them to market their securities and to invest their resources in short term paper or in United States securities or to hold them in the form of currency. Therefore, the yields of bonds fluctuated in the same manner as the yields of stocks thereafter. Rates ruling in short term markets remained low due to the changing investment demands and to the easy money policy of the Federal Reserve System.

SUMMARY

A comparison of rates of interest ruling in the money and capital markets for the period since the close of the World War indicates that their variations are not uniform, but fall into several categories. These categories are the short term markets, the long term markets for obligations with a fixed rate of return, the long term markets for common stocks and the market for government bonds. In the first group are included both short term open market rates of interest and rates charged by banks to those of their customers who are able to obtain accommodation from more than one source. In the second are all fixed interest bonds and preferred stocks. In the third group are all common stocks. In the fourth group are those securities in which the Reserve banks have dealt extensively.

Rates ruling in the short term markets are subject to a high degree of influence by factors affecting the supply of available loanable funds, such as Reserve bank operations in the money market. The rates which Federal Reserve banks charge for rediscounting do not affect the rates ruling in short term markets because banks borrow only to rectify their reserve positions; and the rates which they pay, therefore, apply only to their marginal funds.

The irregularities of rate movements in the money and capital markets set up limitations to the effectiveness of Federal Reserve policy. Operations of the Reserve banks can cause changes in the rate of interest on all funds borrowed only at times when there is no large fund of money in the possession of investors outside of the banking system. Irregularities in rate movements cause borrowers to shift their demands from one market to another if they can do so. The extent to which borrowers can make such shifts and the effect which changing rates of interest have upon their willingness to borrow will be the subject of the next chapter.

CHAPTER VIII

INTEREST RATE CHANGES AND THE FLOW OF CREDIT

HAVING established that the operations of the Reserve banks have a direct effect upon interest rates ruling in short term money markets and upon the yields of government bonds, though not upon the yields of other long term securities, we can prove that Federal Reserve policy is effective in controlling the rate of credit extension if high rates in these markets are associated with scant borrowing and vice versa. An examination of the effects of changing interest rates upon the rate of borrowing will be the subject of this chapter.

THE SIGNIFICANCE OF RATE CHANGES

The significance of changes in interest rates and particularly of changes in rate differentials lies in the effects which they have upon the borrowing operations of businesses and upon the investment choices of lenders. Other things being equal, borrowers will choose that market in which the lowest rates rule, while lenders will prefer high rate markets. But the inclusion of the risk element in shaping the direction of investment of lenders will cause them to shun high rate markets at times of uncertainty. At other times the opportunity of gaining high returns by speculative purchases and resales will cause them to prefer a low rate market, even though they have to borrow in a high rate market in order to exercise this choice. These processes widen the differentials between rates ruling in different markets at times when great social unrest or speculative activity are the rule. This differential, then, may be a greater one than can be explained on the orthodox theory of risk.

If the effect of changes in rates upon the investment choices of lenders are not the same in all markets the automatic checks bringing about a return to equilibrium may not act and rate differentials will continue to increase rather than to decrease.

Some borrowers are influenced more by rate considerations than are others. The same holds true of lenders. If a borrower may have access to more than one market he chooses that one in which rates ruling are low. But borrowers who do not have access to more than one market must raise money in the accustomed channels whatever the cost, unless they do not borrow at all. At one extreme stand the larger corporations which have the option of issuing new stocks, floating new bonds or borrowing in short term markets. At the other extreme stand brokers, who must borrow on collateral from banks or other lenders at the rate ruling in the call loan market or not borrow at all. Small business borrowers, foreign borrowers, etc., also borrow in more limited markets at any rate which prevails. Foreign borrowers have had the option, in recent years, of floating long term bonds or of borrowing from banks through the medium of the bankers' acceptance market. Their choice was limited less by the rate of interest than by the availability of these markets. This subject was treated in Chapter V. Lenders are also less influenced by rate considerations in some markets than in others. A rise in security yields may be a signal of danger and repel new funds, while a rise in the call loan rate may attract them.

INTEREST RATES AND BORROWING ACTIVITY IN VARIOUS MARKETS

In order to determine the effect of rates of interest on the amount of new credit extended in the various markets, the yields of various securities or kinds of loans were compared with the new credit in those markets. In the cases of the markets for long term funds, the comparison was made with new issues of securities. In the cases of short term markets, since old loans are constantly maturing, the total amount of credit extended which is outstanding was used as a basis of comparison. In the case of brokers' loans no distinction

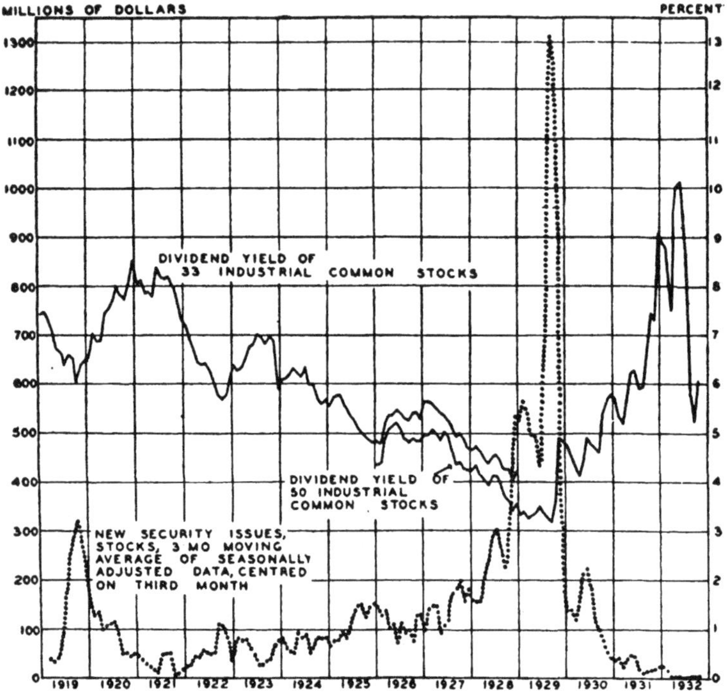

CHART 16. YIELDS OF INDUSTRIAL COMMON STOCKS COMPARED WITH NEW ISSUES OF STOCKS

Data on yields from Standard Statistics Co.
Data on New Issues from *Commercial and Financial Chronicle*

was made between time and demand loans and the call loan rate rather than the time loan rate was chosen. The majority of loans made are made on demand and the call loan rate is the rate which affects the marginal credit extended in this market.

Supply and Demand Curves for Money and Capital Markets

Charts 16 through 20 show the relationship between the rates charged and the new credit extended in the various markets for which data are readily available. In the case of common stocks, any decline in the yield has invariably been accompanied by an increase in the amount of new issues and *vice versa.* This was the case for bonds only after 1924, indicating that there was a change in underlying conditions at that time. After 1924, in periods when new stock issues were low new bonds were issued in larger amounts. Before that time, when new stock issues declined, new issues of bonds increased somewhat, though not proportionately to the decline in new issues of stocks.

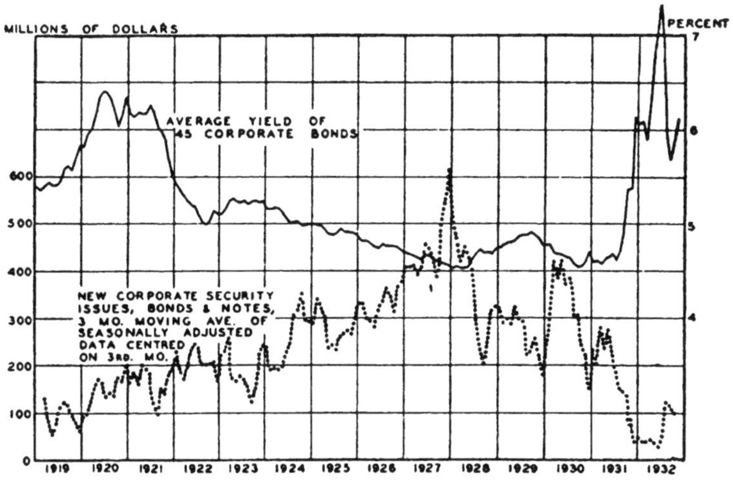

CHART 17. YIELDS OF CORPORATE BONDS COMPARED WITH NEW ISSUES OF BONDS

Data on yields from Standard Statistics Co.
Data on new issues from *Commercial and Financial Chronicle*

The amount of commercial paper outstanding was ruled by the rate between the years 1924 and 1930. Before and

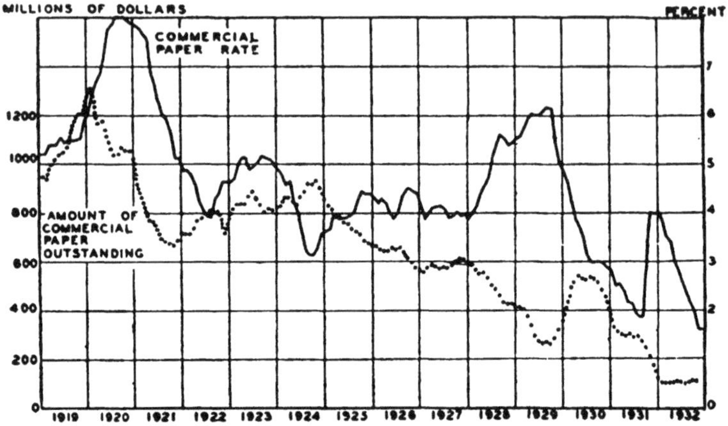

CHART 18. THE COMMERCIAL PAPER RATE COMPARED WITH THE VOLUME OF COMMERCIAL PAPER OUTSTANDING

Data on Volume Outstanding from Federal Reserve Bank of New York
Data on Rates from Standard Statistics Co.

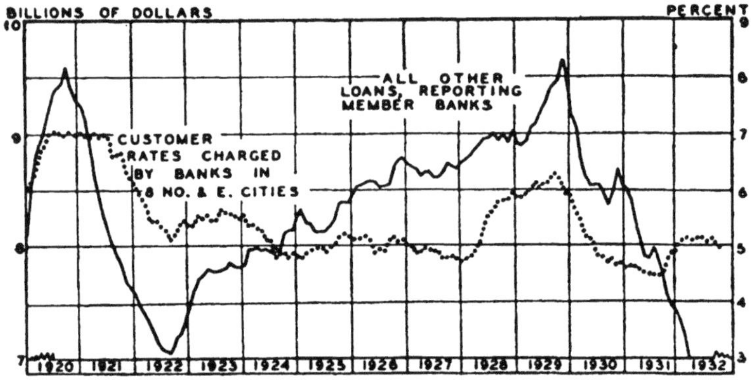

CHART 19. UNSECURED LOANS BY REPORTING MEMBER BANKS OUTSIDE NEW YORK CITY COMPARED WITH RATES CHARGED ON PRIME COMMERCIAL LOANS BY BANKS IN EIGHT NORTHERN AND EASTERN CITIES OTHER THAN NEW YORK CITY

Data from Federal Reserve Board

after that date, factors independent of the rate had more influence on the volume in use. In the case of commercial loans at banks,[1] there was a lack of relationship throughout

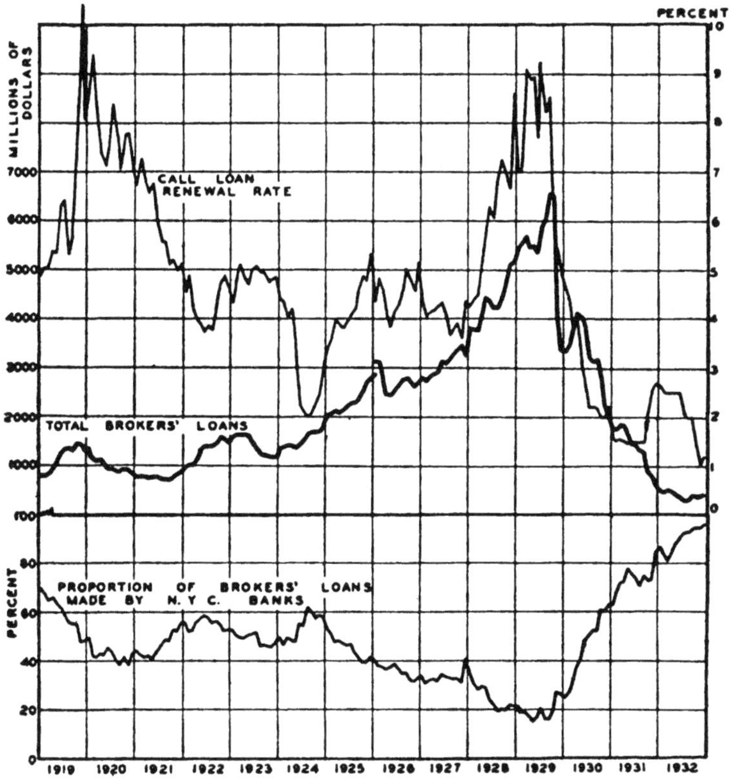

CHART 20. LOANS TO BROKERS COMPARED WITH CALL LOAN RENEWAL RATES AND THE PROPORTION OF BROKERS' LOANS MADE BY NEW YORK CITY BANKS

Data from Federal Reserve Board

[1] "All other loans" of reporting member banks outside New York City are taken as being representative of commercial loans at banks, in respect to variations, if not to actual amounts. These loans represent all loans other than those secured by stocks and bonds. Therefore, there is some overlapping with other categories of loans, particularly with

the whole period. When the data are broken up into periods, however, it may be seen that loans at banks increased with increasing interest rates and decreased with decreasing rates between 1919 and 1921 and again between 1925 and 1931, while there was a lack of any discernable relationship at other times.

In the case of loans to brokers, considerable study has already been made in Chapter VI of the relation of the rates ruling on them to the amount outstanding in the case of loans by different groups of lenders. It was found that in the cases of loans by banks outside New York City and of loans by others than banks, high call loan rates were a factor causing, not a decrease in borrowing in this market, but an increase in offers of funds. In the case of loans made by New York City banks with their own funds, more loans were made at times when there was easy money or when rates were low, than at times when rates were high. Thus, when the total of loans to brokers is made up principally of loans by banks outside New York or by others than banks, the rate ruling determines the supply of money available and rates rise as new loans rise. When the total is made up for the most part of loans by New York City banks, the reverse holds true. Dividing the data into periods, we find that the funds of others than New York City banks were important between 1919 and 1921 and again between 1925 and 1930. In other years, the total of brokers' loans showed

open market paper discounted. But since other data for commercial loans at banks are for call dates only, in order to find month to month changes it is necessary to use these data. The error is not great, due to the fact that commercial loans held by banks making them are very much larger in amount than open market loans of banks. For the rates ruling in this market, the rates on an average of prime commercial loans and security loans at selected banks in eight northern and eastern cities other than New York was used because this rate is sufficiently representative and is not too heavily weighted by rates on security loans, as are rates for New York City.

but little relationship to the call loan rate. During the periods of declining rates in 1924 and 1927, the loans by New York City banks were a large part of the total and brokers' loans increased with declining rates. But this evidence, for two short periods of time, should not be construed as meaning that the low rates caused a desire to speculate at those times. Low rates and surplus funds in New York City were two common results of the easy money policies of the Federal Reserve System. The relationship between rates in the call loan market and the total amount borrowed by brokers depends upon the proportion of loans by others than New York City banks in the total, and not upon the desire of borrowers to increase their activities when funds are cheap.

Charts 21, 22 and 23 are repititions of the data on Charts 16 through 20 taking no account of the time factor. When the dots on these charts describe a curve which rises toward the right, or a curve of positive slope as the mathematicians would express it, high rates of interest are associated with more borrowing. When the dots describe a curve which declines toward the right, or a curve of negative slope, low rates are associated with more borrowing. The latter type of curve is the conventional demand curve of classical economics. Lower prices bring more demands. The former type of curve, on the other hand, is the supply curve of classical economics. Higher prices bring more funds to be loaned. The markets for stocks and bonds are the only markets in which demand is the controlling factor. That is, when yields are low, corporations issue more securities. But the open market for commercial paper exhibits a demand curve during part of its history—the years 1924 through 1930. The remaining markets show either a lack of any definite relationship or a supply relationship at all times. These curves bear out the contention made in the opening section of this chapter that it is only in markets whose borrowers can exercise choice in determining where to turn for funds that the rate of interest has any effect upon the amount of credit extended.

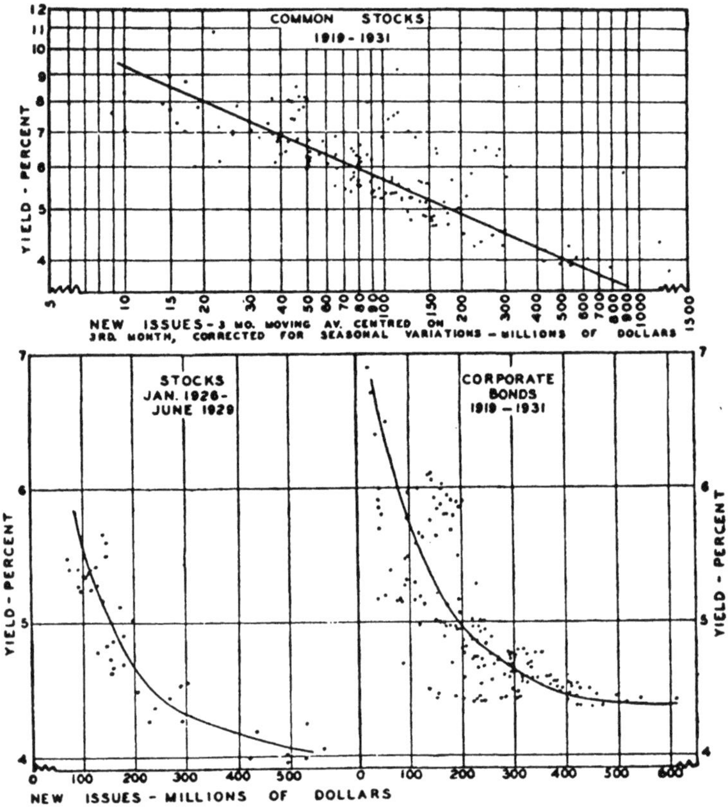

CHART 21. DEMAND CURVES FOR STOCKS AND BONDS

The Effectiveness of Federal Reserve Operations in Various Markets

The theory that the Federal Reserve System may control the amount of credit extended through the effect which it has upon the rate of interest assumes that there is a demand curve describing the relationship between the rate of interest and the amount of borrowing in every market. If such were the case, increases in the rate of interest, brought about through open market operations of the Federal Reserve System, would bring about decreases in the offerings of credit to lenders. A second condition necessary for control of the flow of credit through the mechanism of changes in

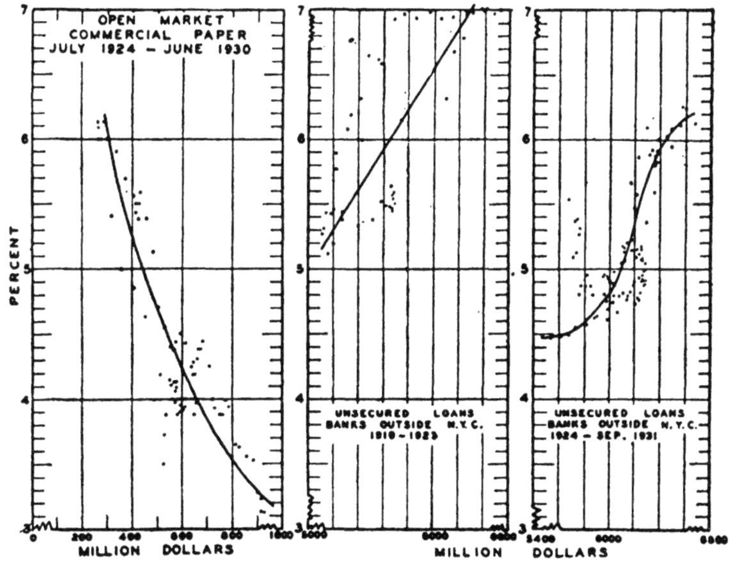

CHART 22. DEMAND CURVES FOR COMMERCIAL PAPER AND COMMERCIAL LOANS OF BANKS OUTSIDE NEW YORK CITY

the rate of interest is that the Federal Reserve System must have the power to influence all interest rates. It has already been demonstrated in the preceding chapter that the Federal Reserve System, through its open market operations, has been able to influence rates of interest in the short term markets only. But it has further been demonstrated in this chapter that rates of interest have influenced the demand for funds only in the long term markets. Therefore, it can readily be seen that the ability of the Federal Reserve System to use the rate of interest to influence the volume of credit extended has been very limited. What these limita-

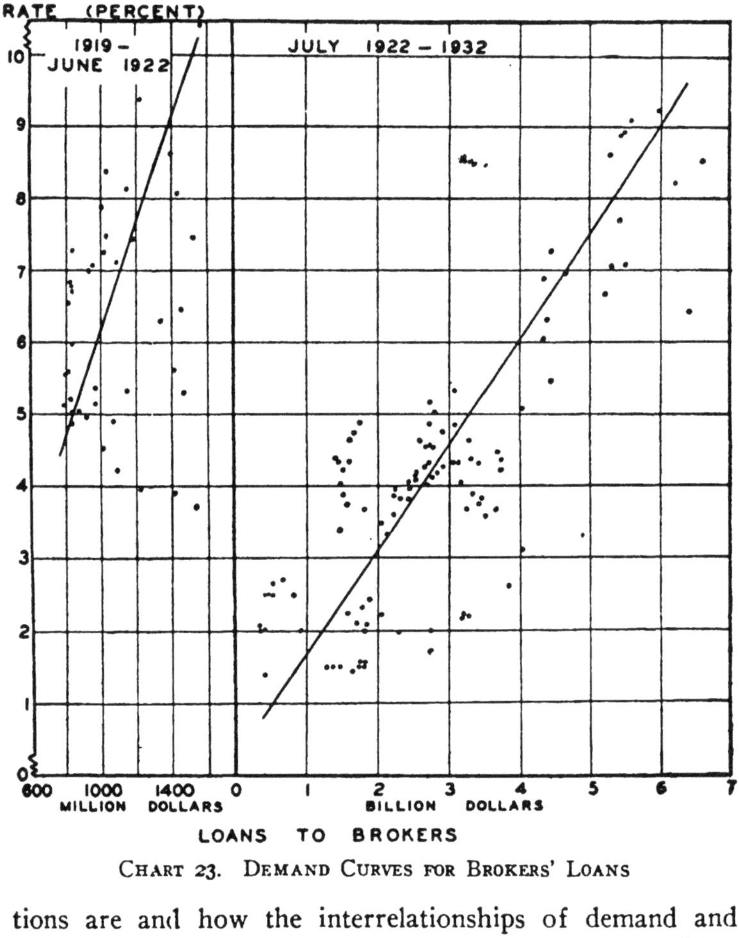

CHART 23. DEMAND CURVES FOR BROKERS' LOANS

tions are and how the interrelationships of demand and supply in the various markets have brought about a condition which was beyond the control of the Reserve banks can be demonstrated.

INTERRELATIONSHIPS BETWEEN MARKETS

When there are interrelationships between markets, either from the demand side or from the supply side, the type of relationship between the rate of interest and the amount of borrowing assumes great significance. Any tendency setting up rate differentials between a market where there is a supply relationship and a market where there is a demand relationship may have grave consequences. Examples of such markets are the brokers' loan market and the markets for long term stocks and bonds. Both supply purchasing power to the large corporations, the former indirectly and the latter two directly. Borrowers in the brokers' loan markets are lenders in the capital markets. If the rate differential be in favor of the market with a supply relationship, i. e., the brokers' loan market, no great consequences will ensue. The low rate ruling on that market will not stimulate borrowing, except for that part which is loans by New York City banks. The funds are limited and the supplies may be readily exhausted. The high rates in the other markets will result in a decrease of borrowing. Demand will be relatively quiescent. There is such a situation at the time of writing—1933—and new credit extended to banks by the Federal Reserve System is not flowing into speculative channels, because the high yields on securities act as an effective check upon the desire to borrow in the securities markets. The expectation of currency inflation would have to be sufficiently great to cause dividend and interest yields on long term securities to be small in terms of goods, for activity upon the colossal scale of 1929 to be renewed.

But if the differential between rates of interest be in favor of the markets with a demand relationship, i. e., the markets for stocks and bonds, great borrowing activity will take place on those markets. This borrowing, if it outruns the supply of real savings of the community, will result in a demand for loans from brokers and dealers in securities. They must borrow in the call loan market, because there is no other market to which they may turn. This activity in the call loan market raises rates so that outside funds are attracted to it. If, as was the case in 1919, outside funds are scarce, supplies of available purchasing power will be shut off and a readjustment in both markets will take place. In 1920 yields on stocks rose while call loan rates declined until an equilibrium position was attained. As a result of the equilibrium in interest rates on the money and capital markets, corporations which had formerly borrowed through new issues of stocks found no low rate market to which they might turn. Borrowing ceased and a rapid liquidation followed. But in the period between 1925 and 1929 the differential, once established, led to active borrowing in the call loan market to purchase new issues of bonds and later on of stocks which were floated because of the low rates prevailing on them. The fact that the real savings of the country were greater than in 1919 enabled outside lenders to provide the necessary funds for the call loan market as soon as rates had risen sufficiently to attract these funds to it. When the speculative fever had reached its height in 1929 and high call loan rates made that market particularly attractive to outside lenders, corporations and investment trusts borrowed in one market in order to lend the proceeds in the other. This set up a circular flow of newly created purchasing power outside of the control of the banking system. Had security purchasers been buying shares to hold until they could pay for them out of income, instead of to resell them, the process could have continued longer. But the fact that the real income of investors was not large enough to pay off the loans forced them to resell. When such a large part of the public had been drawn in that there were no new investors to whom these securities might be resold, the process came to an inevitable conclusion. The real income of the nation had begun to decline, as indicated by declining production statistics and wage payments, and it was no longer possible to sell low yield securities to anyone.

A comparison of the effect of high call loan rates in 1919 with their effect ten years later indicates a third possible limitation upon the ability of the Federal Reserve System to control credit. This has to do with the amount of money available to the money market from sources outside the control of the Reserve banks and the member banks. When there is but little of such money available, very high call loan rates cannot attract outside funds beyond a certain point. Readjustment takes place more quickly. But when, as was the case in 1928 and 1929, large reserves of money await investment by others than banks, the Reserve banks cannot limit loans to brokers by shutting off the supply of banking funds available to this market. The result of such attempted limitation will be higher call loan rates and a consequently greater attraction of this market for the funds of outsiders.

The relation of these demand curves to the problem of credit control depends upon whether the control be exercised indirectly through the medium of interest rates or directly by varying the amount of credit available. If the indirect means be attempted the control will be limited by three factors. In the first place, it is only effective in those markets where there is a demand relationship so that a rise in rates will limit borrowings. In the second place the action of the Federal Reserve System must be able to influence all interest rates in markets to which the borrowing activity may be shifted. In the third place there must be no source of funds from others than banks.

Between 1919 and 1924 the uniformity of rate movements

prevented any undue recourse for long periods of time to markets which were not directly controlled. After the low point in interest rates in 1922 had been passed divergences between rates ruling in various markets began to appear. The yields of stocks rose faster in 1923 than did other interest rates. A tendency to borrow in short term markets began to appear. Though the Reserve banks in larger centers attempted to tighten credit by raising rates early in 1923 and the System sold government securities, active borrowing in the brokers' loan market continued until the middle of the year. This caused an increased demand for stocks, raising their prices and lowering their yields. In 1924 very low rates ruled on the markets for short term paper of all sorts. Borrowing was shifted from the long term markets to the commercial paper market for a time. It was during these years that the brokers' loan market and the commercial loan market showed a demand relationship. Thus low rates in these markets encouraged borrowing but did not repel lending for low rates ruled in other markets also. Toward the end of the year long-term securities became popular and corporations took advantage of this by increasing their borrowing through the medium of the issuance of bonds.

After 1924 a new and abnormal situation developed in the money markets. The Reserve banks attempted to tighten interest rates by selling securities. The result was a tightening of short term interest rates only. The call loan rate rose faster than other short term rates and outside funds were attracted to this market. The continuation of the decline in yields on long term securities caused corporations to avoid borrowing in the commercial paper market and to turn to the long term markets. Each time when the Federal Reserve System attempted to raise rates by open market sales of securities more outside funds were attracted to Wall Street. When yields on stocks rose for a time in 1926 this was not the result of Federal Reserve policy. The effect of this rise was a transfer of new borrowing to the bond market which had not shared in the fall in prices. When the Reserve banks embarked upon an active open market policy coupled with decreases in the rate of rediscount in 1927, the call loan rate, while slightly depressed, did not fall below the level of rates in the bankers' acceptance market, which it had done in 1924, and brokers' loans continued to increase. The yields on stocks and bonds continued to decline and new borrowing through these media resulted in increasing demands for loans by brokers. This resulted in an increased attractiveness of long term investments, particularly stock investments. The differential in interest rates was set up and no act of the Federal Reserve System was able to right it until the fund of money awaiting investment was exhausted.

During the liquidation period the rate differentials were caused by the higher premium for risk demanded by investors in a period of uncertainty. The markets where the relationships between the rate of interest and the amount of new borrowing were determined by demand were high rate markets while the markets where the relationships were determined by supply were low rate markets. Since Federal Reserve policy was felt only in the safe or low rate markets —markets where a low rate does not act as a stimulus to borrowing—it could have no influence upon the amount of new loans made.

SUMMARY

Differentials between rates ruling in the capital markets and rates ruling in the money markets are explained on the basis of varying choices of investors for different kinds of securities. They were beyond the sphere of influence of the Federal Reserve System, which may only change interest rates from the supply side. Therefore, a change in Federal Reserve policy causes changes in short term interest rates only, except at times when there is a shortage of funds.

The significance of these changes in short term interest rates in their effect upon business borrowing is not very great. Reductions in the rates of interest ruling in short term markets, with the possible exception of the open market for commercial paper, do not bring about increases in the borrowings of business in these markets. Reductions in the rates charged on loans to brokers do not bring about increases in the amount so loaned, except at times when the bulk of loans to brokers are made by New York City banks and when there is an active demand for them. Increases in short term rates of interest do not reduce the borrowing demands of the public, but in the case of loans to brokers by others than New York City banks, increase the supplies of money available for this purpose, if such supplies are obtainable. In the capital markets changes in the rates of interest do cause changes in the borrowing taking place, but the Federal Reserve System has no control over rates ruling in these markets at times when investors are possessed of funds obtained from other sources than member banks. Therefore, Federal Reserve policy, while it may cause changes in short term rates of interest, cannot influence the amount of credit used by business.

CHAPTER IX

Federal Reserve Policy and the Problem of Liquidity

The Federal Reserve System, in its attempts to regulate the supply of credit recognized by different leading agencies, has found itself to be an ineffective agency of control. The ineffectiveness of the Federal Reserve System, as previously pointed out, grows out of the fact that it cannot dictate the groups to whom banks extend credit on the basis of reserves added by the System's operations. The System, furthermore, is unable to limit borrowings of favored groups by raising the rate of interest ruling on the money markets, because it cannot influence rates of interest on the capital markets, where favored borrowers may also turn for funds. The rates of interest ruling on capital markets would not be of interest to the banking system if bank funds were not used on these markets. But since speculative loan markets provide channels through which bank funds go to capital markets, and hence to industry, the System must be able to regulate bank funds going to speculative loan markets, in order to regulate business borrowing. The rate of interest is not a means of doing this, since security operators are as willing to borrow at high rates as at low rates. The suggestion is often heard that the Reserve banks dealing in speculative loan paper would not cut off funds from these markets, but would increase the amount already available. Moral suasion was equally ineffective in bringing about regulation of the security loan markets because it was applied after the evil had been done and the loans which it was intended to curb were already made. Since these loans were illiquid and could not be repaid except from the proceeds of new loans, no reduction in the total volume of security loans ensued.

If the Federal Reserve System were able to limit the original lending activities of member banks to liquid loans, it would not have to depend upon credit control to rectify bad situations, previously established. Following the state of trade as a guide to credit policies and using these policies to aid business has resulted in confusion because the Federal Reserve System is unable to influence business when business has so many ways of circumventing its policies. The System should rather limit its activities to the maintenance of the welfare of its stockholders—the member banks. If it tries to avoid situations before they arise, rather than to rectify situations which have arisen, it may incidentally restrain business.

The theory of automatic elasticity, upon which the Federal Reserve Act was founded, assumes that commercial bank credit will be used for commercial purposes only. If commercial bank credit is extended for other uses, the elasticity of the System breaks down, and conscious control must be substituted for automatic control. How ineffective conscious control is has been demonstrated by the history of Federal Reserve policies since the close of the World War. Control was instituted in each case after the damage had been done. To exercise control, the System must be guided by the liquidity of banks and not by secondary effects of credit expansion which come later on, such as the state of trade or the price level. If banks are forced to remain liquid, automatic control will be reinstated.

LIQUIDITY

A bank must estimate the value of the rights to credit of its borrowers. When such a right to credit is recognized, the borrower is put in possession of a larger volume of purchasing power than formerly and there is a change in the distribution of income. At the time of repayment the borrower returns the purchasing power formerly granted to him to the bank, which extinguishes it, cancelling the loan. There is then another change in the distribution of income, lessening the share of the borrower to the same extent as his share was formerly increased.

If a bank recognizes rights to credit which do not exist, the borrower will not repay the loan upon demand or at maturity, and it must be renewed. The change in the distribution of income, resulting from the extension of added purchasing power to the borrower, takes on a more permanent aspect and the bank has had a share in permitting this process to go on. Even though the loan is repaid to the bank which originally made it, but is repaid out of the proceeds of another loan, the change in the distribution of income persists, for purchasing power created by banks as a whole has not declined. The bank making an illiquid loan may be forced to pay for its error in its own insolvency in case creditors of the borrower to whom it has assigned rights against itself demand the conversion of these rights into other means of purchasing goods, such as gold or currency or claims on other banks.[1]

Liquidity of a Loan

Liquidity may be defined as that quality of a loan which insures that it does not result in permanent alterations in the distribution of income. Loans resulting from recognition of true rights of credit are liquid. Loans resulting from the recognition of rights to credit which do not exist are illiquid. Errors of judgment on the part of bankers may be expected

[1] Professor Steiner refers to this process as having caused the failure of Baring Bros. in 1890 and of the Bank of United States in 1930. *Money and Banking*, N. Y., 1933, p. 113, n. 11.

and, consequently, loans possess varying degrees of liquidity. But there are types of loans which are more likely to be liquid than are other types.

Since liquidity depends ultimately upon the salability of goods, a greater degree of liquidity is obtainable where the loan represents goods whose salability can be readily foreseen. Loans for financing the shipment of and payment for goods already sold are, therefore, the most liquid. Loans for providing the means of manufacture are frequently liquid also. Some goods are manufactured to order, others at the will of men whose judgments of the market for their products are sound. Loans for the purpose of acquiring ownership of the means of production, whose use will not provide the means of repayment of the entire amount borrowed at maturity, are illiquid. Such loans are frequently made pending the flotation of a bond issue. Loans in anticipation of a bond issue depend for their liquidity upon the ability of investors to absorb the bond issue out of their savings. Therefore, their liquidity depends upon a knowledge of factors which are but distantly related to the purpose for which the loan has been made, and errors of judgment are frequent. Loans to investors to purchase securities in order to resell them at a profit are probably the most illiquid loans, for repayment depends upon the existence at some future time of more than the present number of investors, anxious to purchase the securities out of income, rather than out of the proceeds of new bank loans. If these investors are certain to exist in the future, why do they not exist in the present? Banks frequently make such loans with the knowledge that they can be liquidated only from the proceeds of new loans either to the original security purchaser or to those to whom he sells. In such cases they are acting single handed, expecting to maintain their own liquidity at the expense of the liquidity of less cautious banks.

Liquidity of Banks

The liquidity of banks is measured by the proportion of their demand and short term time liabilities which were created by the recognition of rights to credit which were valid, i. e., liquid loans. This concept must not be confused with solvency, or the ability to maintain itself solvent, which is a function of the cash position of the bank and of its ability to obtain accretions to its cash reserve.

If banks made only liquid loans, there would be a limitation of the volume of purchasing power created by banks to the value of goods in the process of production or of marketing at the current price. For purchasing power arises from two sources, the possession of exchangeable resources by the people and the loans made by banks. If the loans made by banks are limited to the volume of exchangeable goods at a conservative valuation, less a small amount to be held in the form of cash or its equivalent by borrowers to insure their solvency, total purchasing power outstanding will not exceed the value of exchangeable goods in volume. Therefore, the limitation of bank loans to liquid loans, while diminishing the size of banks, would remove the necessity for the exercise of quantitative credit control—a form of control which has never been successfully applied.

Shiftability as a Basis for Liquidity

The shiftability principle, as contrasted to the liquidity principle has been generally used by banks as a guide to safety. The shiftability principle assumes that any loans are as safe as are liquid loans, if they can be shifted to other banks. The principle is safe as applied to an individual bank, provided other banks are willing to take over the shiftable loans, but not to banks as a whole. At a time when banks were anxious to expand illiquid credit, a number of apologists for shiftability arose to justify the prevailing practice. Among these was Waldo F. Mitchell, whose book, *The Uses of Bank Funds,* attracted attention. He stated:[2]

> There have been two theories of the liquidity of bank earning assets, as applied to an individual bank. First, there is what may be called the "orthodox" theory, which states that banks should loan only for short periods of time for commercial purposes, so that the maturing of the paper would complete the commercial transaction and liquidate the loans. The second theory may be called the "shiftability" theory. This second holds that experience shows that paper often cannot be liquidated at maturity, it may not be desirable to liquidate it; that when demand is made on the liabilities of an individual bank, the only reliance for liquidity in an emergency lies in the power to shift assets to other banks and get funds from the banks that still have available funds; and that when credit has been largely expanded and assets have been shifted until the reserves are practically exhausted in all the banks, liquidity in the banking system can be attained only by a slowing up of business or a lowering of the price level. This showing up of business or lowering of the price level will permit a decrease in bank loans, after a time, and thus will relieve the exhausted reserves.

The dependence of the banks upon the principle of shiftability for the liquidity of their loans has forced upon the Reserve banks two courses of action. In the first place, they have had to exercise quantitative credit control to prevent the occurrence of a situation where reserves are practically exhausted. The failure of their program of quantitative credit control resulted in the collapse of the banking system in 1933. In the second place, they are forced to maintain themselves in a position of very great liquidity, since it is to the Reserve banks that member banks shift their assets in times of emergency.

[2] Waldo F. Mitchell, *The Uses of Bank Funds*, Chicago, 1925, p. 3.

Adherents to the shiftability principle may be split into two schools. One group holds that a bank may safely invest its assets in non-self-liquidating loans if they are secured by collateral for which there is a ready market outside of the banking system. This might be called the marketability principle. It justifies loans on securities or on the collateral of readily marketable goods, whatever their purpose, provided the loans are amply secured by a pledge of the securities or the goods. It is assumed that in times of need the banks may recover the value of illiquid loans by selling the collateral behind them to investors outside of the banking field. It will operate safely only in times when outside investors are possessed of cash resources sufficient to absorb the sales by banks. This puts a limit on the amounts which banks may lend in this manner. It has been demonstrated in an earlier chapter that banks over-loaned on security collateral to brokers during each period of boom since data on brokers' loans have been available. In subsequent periods of decline they were unable to realize upon these loans without increasing their loans on securities to customers. The market could not absorb the selling caused by the calling of loans to brokers without price declines of such magnitude that the banks would realize less from security sales than the values of the loans which they had made. Wheat and cotton loans were also not realized upon in periods of price decline. Therefore, the fact that banks periodically exceed the safe limits to loans on the security of marketable collateral makes it desirable that there should be some control, either direct or indirect, of the amount of such loans.

A second variant of the shiftability theory holds that a bank's assets are safe if loaned in such a form that they may be shifted from weaker banks to other and stronger banks in times of need. Because the panic of 1907 demonstrated that there could be times when no banks were in a strong position, the Federal Reserve System was formed, in order that the Reserve banks might take over the better assets of any bank in times of need, due to a crisis or to seasonal strain causing undue demands for currency. The liquidity of an individual bank is measured today by most bankers by the proportion which its cash and assets of types which may be rediscounted at the Reserve banks represents of its deposit liabilities. This measure of liquidity obviously is not adequate for it assumes that the Federal Reserve banks are in a condition of 100 percent liquidity and can always provide currency or reserves in return for assets rediscounted. Illustrative of this point of view is the opinion given in a recent publication of the National Industrial Conference Board: "In plain language banking liquidity means the ready convertibility at any particular moment of banking assets into cash." [3] Among the assets of a bank possessing liquidity in the greatest degree issues of the United States Government are given first place by the Conference Board. The reason is that they may be used as collateral for direct bank borrowing from the Reserve banks. In the second place it mentions commercial loans of a type which may be rediscounted at the Reserve banks.

Liquidity of Federal Reserve Banks

The Federal Reserve Act attempted to restrict paper eligible for rediscount at the Reserve banks to paper which is liquid according to the orthodox theory. This means that they should shun investments in the capital market or loans made for the purpose of enabling the borrowers to invest in this market. The funds of the Reserve banks were to be used more directly to finance the needs of commerce and agriculture. The paper which a Federal Reserve bank

[3] Natl. Ind. Conf. Bd., *The Banking Situation in the United States*, N. Y., 1932, p. 76.

might rediscount or buy in the open market was limited by the provisions of sections 13 and 14 of the Federal Reserve Act to " notes, drafts and bills of exchange issued or drawn for agricultural, industrial or commercial purposes, or the proceeds of which have been used, or are to be used, for such purposes."[4] " Notes, drafts or bills covering merely investments or issued or drawn for the purpose of carrying or trading in stocks, bonds or other investment securities, except bonds and notes of the Government of the United States."[5] were expressly prohibited. These instruments, if rediscounted, must have a majority at the time of rediscount of not over 90 days, except that agricultural paper may run up to six months. The maturity of agricultural paper was extended to nine months by the Agricultural Credits Act of 1923. The limitation on maturities was to add the guarantee that credit extended by the Reserve banks should be for a period of time not greater than the customary credit period ruling in industry and in agriculture. Bankers' acceptances, to be eligible for acceptance by member banks or rediscount at or purchase by Reserve banks, were limited to those based on the importation or the exportation of goods with a maturity at the time of acceptance of not over six months and at the time of rediscount or purchase by Reserve banks of not over three months.[6] The Federal Reserve Board, in a ruling published in 1921, interpreted the meaning of section 13 as follows:[7]

The purpose of this requirement is to limit the class of paper which Federal Reserve banks may rediscount to that which is " liquid "—that is, paper which is issued or drawn under such

[4] *Federal Reserve Act*, as originally enacted into law, sec. 13, par. 2, sec. 14, par. 1.

[5] *Federal Reserve Act*, as originally enacted into law, sec. 13, par. 2.

[6] *Federal Reserve Act*, as originally enacted into law, sec. 13, par. 3.

[7] *Federal Reserve Bulletin*, 1921, p. 1079.

circumstances that in the normal course of business there will automatically come into existence a fund available to liquidate each piece of paper, that fund being the final proceeds of the transaction out of which the paper arose.

The other assets of the Federal Reserve banks were to be invested in gold[8] and in bonds and notes of the United States Government and tax anticipation warrants with a maturity of less than six months issued by States, counties, municipalities, etc.[9] Of these investments the government bonds and notes were to be the only illiquid assets, other than banking premises, to be held by the Reserve banks. Thus, it was planned that the twelve Federal Reserve banks should, by their great liquidity in the orthodox sense, be in a position to support the commercial banks of the country in times of need or of seasonal strain, since these latter had adjusted their portfolios to the needs of a liquidity based on the shiftability theory.

To insure that the currency handled by the people and given in payment for goods sold in their final form should have a better backing than other bank liabilities, it was provided that Federal Reserve notes should be backed by gold (a minimum of 40 percent) and by self-liquidating commercial paper (the remainder, 60 percent or less). It was hoped that the national bank notes might soon be retired, but their continuance in use has not been viewed with alarm because they have become a small proportion of the total currency in circulation. Currency issued by the United States Treasury is backed by a larger proportion of gold than Federal Reserve notes and so is liquid. It may be objected that the purpose of the self-liquidating collateral backing

[8] *Federal Reserve Act*, as originally enacted into law, sec. 14(a). At present the Reserve banks invest, not in gold, but in gold certificates issued by the Treasury.

[9] *Federal Reserve Act*, as originally enacted into law, sec. 14 (b).

for Federal Reserve notes was to provide elasticity rather than liquidity and convertibility. In fact, the title of the Federal Reserve Act reads, " An Act to . . . furnish an elastic currency, . . ." But it may be shown that elasticity and liquidity are one and the same thing in practice. Elasticity means the ability to increase under tension with the reciprocal property of a corresponding decrease when the tension is relaxed. Notes which are backed by self-liquidating paper are issued at times when a need arises due to a growth in the number of self-liquidating transactions. Needs for currency for other purposes—i.e., hoarding or speculation—cannot be filled unless the people use their own cash resources for the purpose, or the Reserve banks possess excess gold reserves and can back the notes largely by gold. Demands on the banks for loans for these purposes will, therefore, result in higher interest rates and consequent contraction. But a decline in self-liquidating transactions involves a decline in the need for currency on the part of final consumers. As the transactions have been truly self-liquidating the borrowers will come into possession of the additional currency before their loans mature or at maturity. Then the back flow of currency through them to the banks and through the banks to the Reserve banks will commence.

Deposit liabilities of the Reserve banks, most of which consist of member bank reserve balances, are backed partly by gold (a minimum of 35 percent) and the remainder by government bonds or commercial paper. Thus, it is possible to have a deposit inflation resulting in greater illiquidity of the Reserve banks than would be possible if currency were in demand also. In the early years of the operation of the Federal Reserve System such a possibility was not foreseen because it was assumed that an inflation of deposits would bring with it a need for currency and that the result would be a growing need for additional member bank advances or rediscounts from the Reserve banks. These could only be increased by an increase in available banking assets of a type which can be rediscounted at the Reserve banks. If these were limited to self-liquidating paper, this need would make the banks tend to put pressure upon borrowers who were contemplating investment or speculative transactions in order to be able to accommodate those who were contemplating commercial transactions.

The adjustments to an undue expansion foreseen in this process may be hindered by several contingencies. First, borrowers who contemplate non-commercial transactions may be able to consummate their business affairs without increasing the need of the public for currency. If the banks possess sufficient illiquid assets of a type which may be rediscounted at the Reserve banks, even though they may not be used for collateral behind Federal Reserve notes, no check to the expansion occurs. Speculative transactions, which are completed by the use of checks rather than cash, may continue on the basis of limited reserves. A time such as the decade following the war, when United States Government securities are outstanding in large amounts and available as a basis for member bank reserves, is particularly ripe for such inflation. Between the years 1925 and 1929 there was a continuous decline in currency in circulation in spite of the fact that deposits of banks were rising. To the extent that deposit liabilities of banks rose while assets of the Reserve banks took the form of United States Government securities, there was a growing danger that any new development causing the public to desire to withdraw bank balances in cash would cause a strain on the Reserve banks. In the second place, at times when deposit liabilities of banks are increasing due to a greater demand for illiquid loans, the Reserve banks may artificially provide their member banks with surplus reserves by the purchase of illiquid assets in the open market. Such purchases result in a lowering of market rates of interest and a consequent lowering of the incentive to banks to limit their non-liquid loans. This process has been often repeated between 1924 and 1932, with the result that when the Reserve banks were called upon, during 1931 and 1932, to provide excess currency, they did not have sufficient liquid assets other than gold to back the currency. In the third place, the Federal Reserve Board may, by means of rulings and regulations on the exact nature of eligible paper, relax its requirements and permit paper which is not truly self-liquidating to be acquired by Reserve banks and used as backing for Federal Reserve notes.

After the passage of the Federal Reserve Act regulations of the Federal Reserve Board defining more closely the paper made eligible by the Act, rulings and opinions of counsel for the Board on the eligibility of specific pieces of paper which appeared to be borderline cases as well as Congressional amendments to the Act changed the position of the Federal Reserve System on the subject of liquidity from time to time. The rulings of the Federal Reserve Board on the nature of drafts which a member bank is allowed to accept defined the kinds of such drafts in existence and had a marked influence on conditions of trade. The early rulings put a strict interpretation upon the meaning of liquidity. Later rulings relaxed this. In 1916 the secured drafts was admitted under an amendment to the Act. After that date more and more emphasis came to be placed on the marketability of the collateral behind the secured draft and less and less on the transaction.

Securities issued by the government of the United States are essentially illiquid. Issued to cover budgetary deficits, they cannot be retired in short periods of time, unless they are issued in anticipation of the receipt of taxes. They do possess shiftability in a high degree at times, especially when commercial banks are in the market for them or when investors are increasing their holdings. But whenever the yield of government bonds is low, investors are unwilling to take them over and these are the times when Reserve banks are in possession of large numbers of such bonds.

Before the World War the government debt consisted largely of a small issue of bonds used as backing for national bank notes. The war increased the debt of the United States government twenty-six fold, from 972 million dollars at the end of the fiscal year, 1916, to 25,234 million dollars at the end of the fiscal year 1919. After this date ten billions of dollars' worth of securities were repaid over a period of ten years. As a result the debt stood at just under sixteen billion dollars in the middle of the year 1930, representing an amount more than sixteen times the pre-war amount. The inability of the United States Government to meet its expenses out of income led to an increase amounting to 3,239 million dollars in the following two years.

In floating these securities the government of the United States depended largely on Reserve bank assistance. The assistance was granted in several ways. First, the Reserve banks purchased securities in the open market. Doing this ostensibly to release credit to trade and industry, they also assisted the government to market its securities at a low rate of interest. Second, the Reserve banks discounted notes secured by the same bonds. These notes were either the notes of customers of banks who had used the proceeds to purchase the securities or of the banks themselves which used the proceeds to rectify their reserve positions, thus being able to purchase more securities. The former type of note was in greater use during and just after the close of the World War although it never exceeded in amount the member bank collateral notes secured by United States Government obligations. The latter was in greater use during the period of credit expansion in 1928 and 1929. Purchase was used during the period of increase in government debt in 1931 and 1932. Table 7 shows the distribution of the earning assets of the Federal Reserve banks between United States Government securities and commercial paper at the middle of each year since the Federal Reserve System was organized. Municipal warrants, because they possess liquidity due to the fact that they are issued in anticipation of taxes, are included with commercial paper. The percentage of Reserve bank earning assets based on commercial loans is an indication of the liquidity of the Reserve banks. But the United States securities obtained as collateral for bills discounted are more liquid than those securities which are purchased outright, due to the fact that the member bank obtaining the discount accommodation is responsible for its repayment. Table 8 gives the bills discounted separated according to underlying security and to whether the advance was on a member bank's note or on a note which it rediscounted.

The liquidity of the Reserve banks was considerably weakened during the war and again during the depression of 1930 to 1933. In 1919 the Reserve banks found themselves in an illiquid condition. They had no supplies of free gold. Pressure upon their reserves served as a signal for contraction. The next time when their liquidity was impaired was during 1922. At that time there was little demand for currency and the Reserve banks had been forced to buy securities in order to earn their expenses and their dividend requirements. The same situation was repeated in 1924. The member banks were in an unusually solvent condition in those years and did not depend upon the Reserve banks for aid so that contraction was not necessary. Between 1927 and 1929 the liquidity of the Reserve banks was again impaired, first through security purchases in 1927 and later

TABLE 7

DISTRIBUTION OF EARNING ASSETS OF FEDERAL RESERVE BANKS IN LIQUID AND ILLIQUID FORMS

Year	*All earning assets*	*U. S. securities rediscounted*	*U. S. securities purchased*	*Total reserve bank credit based on U. S. securities*	*Reserve bank credit based on commercial loans* *
		(millions of dollars)			
June 30, 1915...	56	none	8	8	48
" 30, 1916...	172	none	57	57	115
" 30, 1917...	495	26	71	96	398
" 30, 1918...	1,345	435	259	694	652
" 30, 1919...	2,354	1,573	232	1,805	549
" 30, 1920...	3,183	1,278	352	1,630	1,553
" 30, 1921...	2,051	638	259	897	1,154
" 30, 1922...	1,178	167	555	723	455
" 30, 1923...	1,144	407	102	509	635
" 30, 1924...	803	116	431	547	256
" 30, 1925...	1,100	245	353	599	501
" 30, 1926...	1,158	253	385	638	520
" 30, 1927...	1,025	245	370	615	410
" 30, 1928...	1,548	750	235	985	563
" 30, 1929...	1,347	575	216	791	556
" 30, 1930...	996	108	591	699	297
" 30, 1931...	932	47	668	715	216
" 30, 1932...	2,310	157	1,784	1,940	369
		(percent of total earning assets)			
June 30, 1915...	100.0	0.0	14.3	14.3	85.7
" 30, 1916...	100.0	0.0	33.2	33.2	66.8
" 30, 1917...	100.0	5.2	14.3	19.5	80.5
" 30, 1918...	100.0	32.3	19.3	51.6	48.4
" 30, 1919...	100.0	66.8	9.9	76.7	23.3
" 30, 1920...	100.0	40.2	11.1	51.3	48.7
" 30, 1921...	100.0	31.1	12.6	43.7	56.3
" 30, 1922...	100.0	14.2	47.1	61.3	38.7
" 30, 1923...	100.0	35.6	8.9	44.5	55.5
" 30, 1924...	100.0	14.4	53.7	68.1	31.9
" 30, 1925...	100.0	22.3	32.1	54.4	45.6
" 30, 1926...	100.0	21.8	33.3	55.1	44.9

" 30, 1927...	100.0	23.9	36.1	60.0	40.0
" 30, 1928...	100.0	48.5	15.2	63.7	36.3
" 30, 1929...	100.0	42.7	16.0	58.7	41.3
" 30, 1930...	100.0	10.9	59.4	70.3	29.7
" 30, 1931...	100.0	5.1	71.7	76.8	23.2
" 30, 1932...	100.0	6.8	77.2	84.0	16.0

Source: Fed. Res. Bd., *Annual Reports* and *Fed. Res. Bulletin*.

* Includes commercial and other similar paper rediscounted, municipal warrants, bankers' acceptances, trade acceptances, etc. purchased in the open market.

TABLE 8

BILLS DISCOUNTED AT FEDERAL RESERVE BANKS CLASSIFIED

	Secured by U. S. Gov. Obligations		*Secured by Commercial Paper, etc.*		
End of Year	*Rediscounted paper*	*Member bank collateral notes*	*Member bank collateral notes*	*Rediscounted paper*	*Total*
		(millions of dollars)			
1917	133	151	88	310	681
1918	363	1,037	22	281	1,703
1919	353	1,158	8	676	2,195
1920	272	870	18	1,560	2,719
1921	42	444	18	641	1,144
1922	4	328	10	276	618
1923	4	350	6	363	723
1924	1	186	22	105	314
1925	2	380	72	181	635
1926	1	364	98	174	637
1927	(a)	418	74	89	582
1928	1	658	181	217	1,056
1929	1	353	106	173	632
1930	(a)	89	62	100	251
1931	4	318	102	215	638
1932	1	60	68	91	220
		(percent of total bills discounted)			
1917	19.5	22.2	12.9	45.4	100.0
1918	21.3	60.9	1.3	16.5	100.0
1919	16.1	52.7	0.4	30.8	100.0
1920	10.0	32.0	0.6	57.4	100.0

1921	3.6	38.8	1.6	56.0	100.0
1922	0.6	53.1	1.6	44.7	100.0
1923	0.6	48.4	0.8	50.2	100.0
1924	0.3	59.2	7.0	33.5	100.0
1925	0.3	59.8	11.4	28.5	100.0
1926	0.2	57.1	15.4	27.3	100.0
1927	0.0	71.9	12.8	15.3	100.0
1928	0.1	62.2	17.2	20.5	100.0
1929	0.2	55.8	16.7	27.3	100.0
1930	0.0	35.5	24.7	39.8	100.0
1931	0.6	49.8	16.0	33.6	100.0
1932	0.4	27.3	30.9	41.4	100.0

Source: Federal Reserve Board, *Annual Reports.*

(a) Less than $500,000.

through the discount of member bank collateral notes backed by securities in 1928 and 1929. The fortunate coincidence of a relatively quiescent demand for currency and ample supplies of free gold in Reserve bank vaults enabled the Reserve banks to meet all calls upon them during those years, without fear of the effects of the publication of a low reserve ratio. But too great faith in the continuation of a quiescent public demand for currency left them unprepared for the years that followed.

The depression of 1930 through 1933 saw a rapid impairment of Reserve bank liquidity through large purchases of United States Government securities. Early in 1932, the free gold of the Federal Reserve banks having almost entirely disappeared, it was necessary to pass legislation enabling them to back Federal Reserve notes by government bonds instead of by commercial paper. The stronger member banks were then in a liquid condition while the weaker member banks were in an illiquid condition and depended upon the Reserve banks to supply their currency needs. The Reserve banks were not in a condition to aid them when aid was needed.

The Liquidity of the Portfolios of Banks

Commercial banks were, during the post-war years, increasing the proportion of their liabilities which was represented by illiquid loans and investments. The extent to which they ignored the need for liquidity is shown in Tables 9, 10 and 11. From Table 9 it is evident that, with the exception of the year 1919, when banks held a large part of the newly issued government debt, investments of banks

TABLE 9

LOANS AND INVESTMENTS OF ALL REPORTING BANKS IN THE UNITED STATES, ALASKA AND INSULAR POSSESSIONS

End of June	*Loans*	*Investments*	*Total loans and investments*	*Loans*	*Investments*	*Total loans and investments*
	(millions of dollars)			(percent of total)		
1919.....	25,396	12,230	37,626	67.5	32.5	100.0
1920.....	31,365	11,388	42,753	73.4	26.6	100.0
1921.....	29,014	11,382	40,396	71.8	28.2	100.0
1922.....	27,935	12,548	40,483	69.0	31.0	100.0
1923.....	30,475	13,673	44,148	69.0	31.0	100.0
1924.....	31,484	14,229	45,713	68.9	31.1	100.0
1925.....	33,934	15,400	49,334	68.8	31.2	100.0
1926.....	36,283	15,815	52,098	69.6	30.4	100.0
1927.....	37,314	17,255	54,569	68.4	31.6	100.0
1928.....	39,592	18,772	58,364	67.8	32.2	100.0
1929.....	41,433	17,349	58,782	70.5	29.5	100.0
1930.....	40,510	17,945	58,455	69.3	30.7	100.0
1931.....	35,210	20,060	55,270	63.7	36.3	100.0
1932.....	28,090	18,223	46,313	60.7	39.3	100.0

Source: U. S. Comptroller of the Currency, *Annual Reports*.

rose faster than did loans. Table 10 shows the distribution of these investments according to type of security. Table 11 shows that in their loan policies banks tended to increase their long term loan or loans the proceeds of which were applied to investment in the capital markets since 1926. Between the close of the World War and 1925 or 1926 loans

TABLE 10

INVESTMENTS OF ALL REPORTING BANKS IN THE UNITED STATES, ALASKA AND INSULAR POSSESSIONS

End of June	*U. S. Gov. securities*	*State, county and municipal bonds*	*R. R. and other public service corp. bonds*	*Other bonds and stocks*	*Total investments*
		(millions of dollars)			
1919	4,162	622	1,262	6,183	12,230
1920	3,344	643	1,674	5,727	11,388
1921	3,872	1,368	2,420	3,722	11,382
1922	3,500	981	2,109	5,957	12,548
1923	4,211	894	2,174	6,394	13,673
1924	4,614	1,401	2,815	5,398	14,229
1925	4,182	1,067	2,745	7,406	15,400
1926	4,060	1,271	2,749	7,734	15,815
1927	3,829	1,724	2,992	8,710	17,255
1928	4,153	1,890	3,322	9,407	18,772
1929	4,023	1,746	3,094	8,485	17,349
1930	3,847	1,702	3,328	9,067	17,945
1931	5,718	2,266	3,868	8,209	20,060
1932	6,456	2,802	4,276	4,690	18,223
		(percent of total investments)			
1919	34.0	5.1	10.3	50.6	100.0
1920	29.4	5.6	14.7	50.3	100.0
1921	34.0	12.0	21.3	32.7	100.0
1922	27.9	7.8	16.8	47.5	100.0
1923	30.8	6.5	15.9	46.8	100.0
1924	32.4	9.8	19.8	38.0	100.0
1925	27.2	6.9	17.8	48.1	100.0
1926	25.7	8.0	17.4	48.9	100.0
1927	22.2	10.0	17.3	50.5	100.0
1928	22.1	10.1	17.7	50.1	100.0
1929	23.2	10.1	17.8	48.9	100.0
1930	21.4	9.5	18.6	50.5	100.0
1931	28.5	11.3	19.3	40.9	100.0
1932	35.4	15.4	23.5	25.7	100.0

Source: U. S. Comptroller of the Currency, *Annual Reports.*

TABLE 11

LOANS OF ALL REPORTING BANKS IN THE UNITED STATES, ALASKA AND INSULAR POSSESSIONS

End of June	*Loans on real estate*	*Loans on collateral*	*All other loans*	*Total loans including overdrafts*
		(millions of dollars)		
1919	2,384	8,146	14,866	25,396
1920	2,558	8,519	20,289	31,365
1921	4,753	7,819	16,442	29,014
1922	3,511	6,635	17,790	27,935
1923	5,054	6,036	19,384	30,475
1924	3,731	5,703	22,049	31,484
1925	2,047	6,625	25,262	33,934
1926	2,748	7,564	25,971	36,283
1927	5,850	7,615	23,849	37,314
1928	6,381	8,723	24,488	39,592
1929	10,420	11,211 *	19,802 *	41,433
1930	10,446	11,533 *	18,531 *	40,510
1931	10,137	9,111 *	15,962 *	35,210
1932	9,942	6,011 *	12,137 *	28,090
		(percent of total loans)		
1919	9.4	32.1	58.5	100.0
1920	8.1	27.2	64.7	100.0
1921	16.4	26.9	56.7	100.0
1922	12.6	23.7	63.7	100.0
1923	16.6	19.8	63.6	100.0
1924	11.9	18.1	70.0	100.0
1925	6.0	19.5	74.5	100.0
1926	7.6	20.8	71.6	100.0
1927	15.7	20.4	63.9	100.0
1928	16.1	22.0	61.9	100.0
1929	25.1	27.1	47.8	100.0
1930	25.8	28.5	45.7	100.0
1931	28.8	25.9	45.3	100.0
1932	35.4	21.4	43.2	100.0

Source: U. S. Comptroller of the Currency, *Annual Reports.*

* Change of basis for classification. Before 1929 loans to banks secured by stocks and bonds as well as loans secured by collateral other than stocks and bonds and real estate are included in the category, "loans on collateral." For 1929 and later years, this group includes only loans secured by stocks and bonds to others than banks.

for commercial purposes were increasing both absolutely and relatively to the amount loaned. After that date there was a rapid rise in less liquid loans—both loans on security collateral and loans on real estate. When the period of liquidation came, loans on real estate were the most resistant to liquidation. Loans for commercial purposes declined first. Loans on security collateral did not commence to decline until late, but at that time they declined rapidly.

SOLVENCY

The extent of a bank's need for cash or cashable assets depends upon the nature of its liabilities. Theoretically demand deposits are the only liabilities of a bank which are convertible into currency without notice. In actual practice time deposits possess this quality. Capital funds of banks are suitable for investment in slow assets.

Demand deposits may be classified into those which are likely to be withdrawn at quick notice and those less likely to be so withdrawn. For example, bankers' deposits, being regarded by the banks making them as a part of their reserve funds, are always subject to rapid withdrawal. The deposits of individuals and corporations are relatively stable in normal times, though ones of small magnitude are more likely to be drawn upon in their entirety than are large deposits.

The Effect of the Federal Reserve System Upon the Solvency of Banks

Before the advent of the Federal Reserve System bankers were forced to hold sufficient currency to meet peak needs unless their correspondent relationships were such that they could borrow temporarily from some other bank. Since there was a tradition against excessive interbank borrowing and since banks could not depend upon their correspondents to furnish currency at quick notice, it was frequently customary for banks to keep large reserves of currency on hand in excess of the amounts required by law. For this reason any diminution of vault cash was an indication of the necessity for retrenchment. The pressure was normally brough to bear first upon the illiquid loans because loans of a self-liquidating character were expected to yield currency at maturity. The situation is reversed if banks do not feel the necessity for retrenchment until after they have loaned to the limit of their resources. Then they must force a liquidation of a part of their loan portfolios, and the liquid loans are the ones most easily called. How the Federal Reserve System has tended to encourage banks to keep on lending after the old danger signals were passed is an outgrowth of the existence of the System and the consequent tendency of banks to depend upon shiftability, rather than upon liquidity, for the maintenance of soundness.

When the Federal Reserve Act was enacted into law the legal minimum reserves were considerably reduced and member banks were given a ready source of currency provided they maintained a supply of eligible assets in excess of their peak requirements. Inasmuch as illiquid assets, such as loans backed by government bonds, were eligible for rediscount at Reserve banks, though not for use as collateral backing for Federal Reserve notes, the responsibility for holding sufficient reserves which could be turned into currency at quick notice was transferred from the commercial banks to the Federal Reserve banks. The member banks no longer felt any inducement to keep their liquid loans a given proportion of their total assets so long as they had loaned money on government securities—these loans being eligible for rediscount at the Reserve banks. It was up to the Reserve banks to see that they had the gold and commercial paper to back Federal Reserve notes which might be required.

The situation was somewhat changed by the passage of the amendment to the Federal Reserve Act of September 7, 1916, permitting the discount at Reserve banks of member banks' own notes collateraled by government bonds or by commercial paper. This amendment made all United States Government bonds held in the investment portfolios of member banks a part of their potential reserves. While it cannot be said that member banks invest in government securities only in order that they may be able to get accommodation from Reserve banks, the possibility of getting loans in this manner has led them to permit a great growth in their deposit liabilities not based on eligible commercial loans. The result of this practice was that banks increased their deposit liabilities without any provision for the transfer of these claims into currency out of their own resources. The Reserve banks had to hold sufficient liquid reserves in gold or in short term commercial paper to meet any increased demand which might arise due to the high deposit liabilities of banks.

Table 12 shows the percentage relation of vault cash to total deposits for both national and state banks each year since 1900. The introduction of the Federal Reserve System decreased vault cash for national banks—all of which are member banks and which represent the majority of member banks. But it left the vault cash of other banks—most of which are non-member banks—about where it had been. After the close of the World War a movement commenced to reduce the vault cash of all banks very sharply below the point which national banks had been maintaining. The nadir was reached in 1929 for national banks and in 1930 for other banks. After this, due to the deposit liquidation which had been taking place, cash holdings became an increasing proportion of deposit liabilities, particularly for national banks. In recent years cash holdings of banks other than national banks has decreased to a point as low as the cash holdings of national banks. The cause operating to bring about this decrease cannot be found in the relations of Federal Reserve banks with their member banks, for the majority of state banks are not member banks. National banks and state member banks held actual cash reserves in excess of those indicated by Table 12 in the form of bal-

TABLE 12

PERCENTAGE RELATION OF VAULT CASH TO TOTAL DEPOSITS

On or about June 30	*National banks* (percent)	*Other banks*	*On or about June 30*	*National banks* (percent)	*Other banks*
1900	14.6	4.5	1917	5.9	4.2
1901	13.4	4.2	1918	2.7	2.8
1902	13.4	4.1	1919	2.7	2.6
1903	12.7	4.2	1920	2.6	2.6
1904	14.2	4.3	1921	2.5	2.4
1905	12.6	4.0	1922	2.0	2.0
1906	12.0	3.9	1923	1.7	1.8
1907	11.6	4.3	1924	1.9	1.9
1908	14.0	5.4	1925	1.8	1.8
1909	13.3	5.4	1926	1.7	1.9
1910	11.9	5.4	1927	1.7	1.8
1911	13.0	5.1	1928	1.4	1.6
1912	12.4	5.0	1929	1.4	1.4
1913	11.9	4.9	1930	1.5	1.4
1914	12.0	4.8	1931	1.7	1.5
1915	9.7	4.9	1932	1.9	1.6
1916	7.5	4.3			

Compiled from U. S. Comptroller of the Currency, *Annual Reports.*

ances at the Federal Reserve banks. Non-member banks evidently considered their balances with member banks to be a part of their cash reserves although they had no assurance that these balances would be invested in such a way that they could be turned into cash at quick notice. The factors influencing this group of banks in reducing its vault cash evidently had to do with the declining demand on the part of the public for currency and the increasing use of checks for making payments—factors which were present and which the banks thought would persist.

Since member banks consider their balances at Federal Reserve banks to be a part of their cash reserve, we must add these balances to their vault cash to determine their true cash position. Due to the additional fact that there is a tradition against continuous borrowing from its Federal Reserve bank by any member bank, that part of its reserve balance which results from this form of borrowing must be treated as a deduction from its cash reserves. The only group of member banks rendering reports in such a form that all of this information can be obtained is the reporting member banks. It must be borne in mind that in drawing conclusions from data applying to this group of banks we are discovering only the condition of the stronger banks in larger places. Chart 24 shows the net cash position of these banks since the close

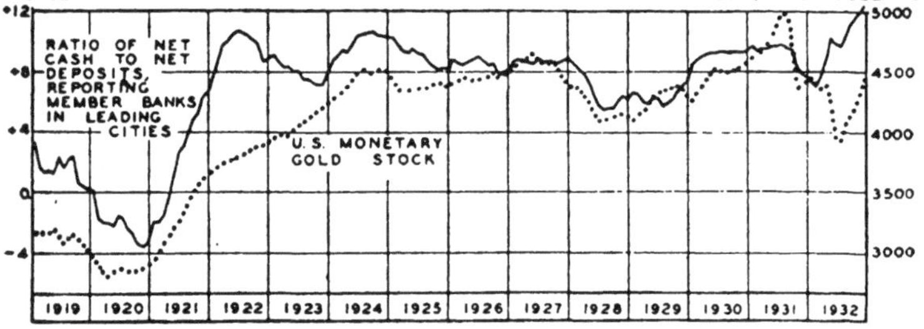

CHART 24. RESERVE POSITION OF REPORTING MEMBER BANKS COMPARED WITH MONETARY GOLD STOCKS

Data on Gold Stocks from Federal Reserve Board

Reserve Position of Reporting Member Banks computed by the author from data of Federal Reserve Board

of the war, expressed as a percentage of net deposits. It can be seen that this percentage corresponds in its major changes to changes in the nation's monetary gold stock. At the most favorable times these member banks held about 9 to 11 percent of their deposits in cash or in the equivalent of cash. During 1920 and the early part of 1921, on the other hand, they were in debt for a greater amount than their total cash holdings. Since this item has shown a continuous increase since that date—a time when vault cash was diminishing—vault cash was in inverse proportion to their liquidity. Therefore, the Federal Reserve banks have during the post war era of gold imports not "sterilized" the excess gold. By holding it they relieved the member banks of the necessity of maintaining as large reserves of vault cash as they would otherwise have held. The first period of gold inflow—from 1921 to 1924—accomplished nothing to stimulate expansion as it was fortunately timed to relieve member banks of a dependence upon Reserve bank assistance which they could not have maintained. Later additions to the gold stock permitted them to expand their loans and, consequently, their deposit liabilities without the necessity of keeping correspondingly increasing reserves of cash. The fact that non-member banks held their vault cash in about the same proportion to their deposits as did member banks introduced instability into their position. Their other reserves consisted, not in deposits in Federal Reserve banks, but in deposits in other commercial banks, which in turn loaned a large percentage of these funds.

SUMMARY

Factors subject to the control of the Federal Reserve Board and the Federal Reserve banks have had little effect upon the solvency of member banks. The fact of the existence of the Federal Reserve banks has reduced their cash holdings, although less than would appear on the surface, for a part of their cash is carried as deposit balances at Federal Reserve banks. The solvency of banks—at least the solvency of the larger member banks in leading cities—has been a function of the monetary gold stocks of the country and not of Federal Reserve policy. Federal Reserve policy has had only an indirect effect upon this insofar as it determined the direction of gold movements.

The liquidity of member banks has been altered by member bank policy during the past eight years. This policy is not directly traceable to the influence of the Federal Reserve System. Easing the regulations upon eligibility of paper has not induced the banks to curtail the creation of liabilities so that their eligible paper would be an increasing proportion of their total loans, even when more paper than formerly was eligible. But the encouragement given to speculative activity by the large open market purchases of the Reserve banks between 1924 and 1930 and the consequent increases in brokers' loans caused banks to lend increasing amounts on security collateral. The inability of banks to force liquidation of these loans brought on the banking crisis which accompanied the depression.

The Federal Reserve banks should try to expel the government bonds held by them even at the cost of increasing the yields on them so that investors would be willing to take them over. Having accomplished this aim, they should pursue one of two courses in the future. They should alter their regulations on the eligibility of paper, putting a stricter interpretation upon that term, at the same time getting legislation passed to eliminate dealings in or loans on government bonds from the System's activities. In such a case the member banks might be entitled to direct their own loan policies depending upon shiftability to the Reserve banks to maintain their solvency. If such drastic action should prove to be impossible, as would probably be the case while the political complexion of the country is what it is today, the System would have to depend upon banking policy, or the supervision of the internal loan policies of member banks, to pursue an effective credit policy.

CHAPTER X

CONCLUSIONS

THE Federal Reserve System of the United States, established in a country with a number of active money markets, must be able to control the volume of borrowing in these markets if it expects its policies to affect business conditions. In view of the fact that the System set out, at the start, not to mitigate the effects of crises, but to do what it could to prevent them, it aims to exercise control over business conditions. For this reason the Federal Reserve System has concentrated its efforts uppn what it calls credit policy. This is carried through to aid borrowers from banks by attempting to make the banks more or less willing to lend according to what is considered the borrowers' welfare. This policy is considered by the Federal Reserve to be more important than banking policy, which has to do with the liquidity of banks, unless there be flagrant abuses of good banking practice, and these are to be dealt with by the bank examiners.

Since banks are many and scattered, the Federal Reserve System was set up on a decentralized plan with semi-independent regional Reserve banks instead of as one central bank with branches, as is the case in all other countries. In controlling markets, it deals directly with its member banks, aiming to alter their reserve positions or to increase the difficulty of their obtaining circulating currency. The Federal Reserve Act also gave the Reserve banks the power of dealing in open money markets within or without their districts, so as to provide an additional tool with which to control the reserve positions of their member banks.

The Federal Reserve System uses various means of controlling the money markets. It may attempt to encourage or to discourage borrowing in specific markets by having the Reserve banks operate in such markets on their own account. In controlling the commercial paper markets—both the open market for commercial paper and the markets for commercial loans to depositors at banks—the System's operations are limited to the rediscount of notes for member banks, undertaken at the request of the member banks. But the member banks may also request to have their own notes secured by government obligations discounted by Reserve banks. By means of their government securities, then, they may obtain access to Reserve banks even though their loans are not eligible; and the power of the System to alter commercial loans through its rediscount powers is useless. The circumvention of Federal Reserve policies by member banks in this respect has been marked since 1922, when member banks commenced to take over a large share of the outstanding interest bearing debt of the United States. In the case of the bankers' acceptance market, created by the Federal Reserve Act, the System has been able to use its power to deal in the market on its own initiative in order to exercise complete control over it. But the Federal Reserve banks have not controlled an outside market, because they were the market. Beginning in 1931, an outside market commenced to develop and this market shows signs of continuing to exist providing the Federal Reserve banks continue their present rate policies. In the case of government securities, the Federal Reserve System does not pretend to regulate the market but to use the purchase and sale of securities as a means of altering the reserve positions of its member banks, in order to encourage or to discourage lending by them. Unfortunately, the type of loan encouraged by security purchases, to date, has been the loan secured by stocks and bonds.

The illiquidity of such loans prevents their contraction at times of security sales by Reserve banks and the member banks are forced by their customers to circumvent the policies of the Reserve banks at such times. Efforts to overcome the unwillingness of the member banks to cooperate with Reserve banks through moral suasion have been applied too late and have been of no value. But provisions of the Banking Act of 1933 requiring that moral suasion, or the refusal to rediscount, be used against banks with overextended security loans may serve in the future to prevent them from undertaking such commitments. Since moral suasion is intended to be exercised only over banks that are in debt to their Reserve banks or that contemplate requesting credit extension, and since illiquid credit extensions by member banks have been undertaken with reserves added through receipts from open market purchases of Reserve banks, open market operations should, in the future, be undertaken upon a much less extended scale.

When the Federal Reserve System attempts to control the rate of borrowing by the indirect method of forcing a change in interest rates, relying upon the assumed effect which changes in interest rates have upon the demand for loans, it is brought face to face with another limitation of ability. In the first place, only rates ruling on short term markets are susceptible to control by the Federal Reserve System's operations. But it is only on the capital markets that the rate of interest influences borrowers. Changes in short term interest rates are not accompanied by the expected change in the demand for loans, for borrowers in these markets have to pay the rate asked or not borrow at all. So far they have shown a disposition to pay such rates, even though they be exorbitant.

The proposal has been made by J. M. Keynes in *The Treatise on Money* that central banks extend their rate control to the capital markets by dealing on a wide scale in long term bonds of the government. The failure of corporate bond yields to conform to the yields of government bonds in their major trends since the close of the World War is proof that the Federal Reserve System would fail in any such attempt if it were tried. To influence the yields of corporate bonds in a predictable manner, the System would have to deal in those bonds whose yields it wished to change. The complexity of a problem involving a large number of issues as well as the danger of the charge of favoritism would render such a course impractical. Furthermore, as previously pointed out, corporate bonds are risky investments and therefore unsuitable for the investment of the primary reserves of commercial banks.

If the Federal Reserve System is as ineffective as it seems to be in controlling the volume of business borrowing, the question naturally arises as to why the System exists and what it can do to mitigate crises. That it can use its elasticity to deaden the shock of a crisis which has already arrived, goes without saying. But to prevent a crisis, it must eradicate the causes of the crisis, particularly the remote ones. If the Federal Reserve System guided its policies with a view to maintaining the liquidity of the member banks, it would be taking a step in the right direction, for as long as member banks remain liquid, no purchasing power will be extended to those without credit. The total volume of purchasing power in existence would approximate the volume of exchangeable goods in the possession of the members of the community and the value of the goods which would shortly come to market at current prices. The Banking Act of 1933, through the powers conferred upon the Federal Reserve Board and the Federal Reserve banks of supervising the collateral loans of member banks, provides a mechanism for such control.

Member banks continually practice unsound policies by acting as individuals and depending upon shiftability of their assets to other banks to replenish exhausted reserves, rather than upon the repayment of loans. They also err by extending credit on the basis of marketability of the collateral at times when there is no market for such collateral except to borrowers from other banks. The Federal Reserve banks have appointed themselves the banks of ultimate resort. To them member banks may shift certain of their assets at times when no other banks can take them. But the Federal Reserve banks did not remain liquid and so had to resort to inflation when the final breakdown came. If member banks had been forced to act individually as they would have acted, had there been but one large member bank rather than many thousands, the necessity for a wholesale shift of assets to the Reserve banks might not have arisen. The Federal Reserve System may have a function in forcing the member banks to maintain themselves in such a condition at all times. This may come to be considered the only true function of the Federal Reserve System. This policy comes under the heading, banking policy, and aims to assist the banks. Its antithesis is credit policy which aims to assist the borrowers from banks. The Banking Act of 1933 provides for control of purchasing power created on the basis of reserves obtained by rediscounting with a view to altering banking policy. Its effects are somewhat lessened by the fact that no control can be exercised over purchasing power created on the basis of reserves obtained from the proceeds of purchases by the Reserve banks of assets bought in the open market. But if banks know that they cannot support their deposit liabilities by rediscounting when the Reserve banks reverse their policies and sell assets in the open market, they are less likely to make illiquid loans, when these assets are purchased.

The automatic elasticity provided for in the Federal Reserve Act, as originally enacted into law, is present in a system which recognizes only commercial credit. Willingness of the Reserve banks to advance funds by other means than the rediscount or purchase of commercial credit instruments has left the ultimate determination of who shall be entitled to bank deposits by borrowing in the hands of member banks. Consequently, the automatic action of the elasticity provided for in the Federal Reserve Act disappeared. Conscious control of credit by men was substituted for it. That this control cannot be exercised by the managers of the member banks has been demonstrated by the history of the past fifteen years. The Federal Reserve System has tried to take over the exercise of control where member banks have failed. The means used were raising rates of interest whenever an undue expansion of illiquid loans had taken place. But the fact that illiquid loans previously contracted do not liquidate easily has forced banks to circumvent the policies of the Federal Reserve System in periods of contraction. The remedy ought rather to be applied before the patient becomes ill. The Federal Reserve System should, though its bank examination apparatus, supervise the leading policies of member banks.

Since it is impossible for the Federal Reserve banks to dictate the use to which the proceeds of their security purchases are applied, they should greatly curtail security purchases in the future. The Banking Act of 1933 has already supplied the mechanism for supervising the security loans of banks which are borrowing on their own notes from their Reserve banks. But borrowing for the purpose of making security loans is not practiced except at times of emergency, and then for short periods of time only. Borrowing from Reserve banks has, in the past, been undertaken to support security credit already recognized. The Banking

Act of 1933 cannot be expected to restrict the speculative tendencies of the American public.

Under a policy of commercial banking, instead of investment banking as at present practiced, banks would be smaller institutions than at present. The volume of bank deposits would be curtailed, but the active parts would remain. The inactive part of bank deposits would seek an outlet in outside investment markets, where it could not be converted into purchasing power until other investors are willing to purchase the underlying securities. The danger of conversion of bank deposits into currency for hoarding purposes would be lessened due to the fact that only the active part of bank deposits could be so converted. This active part must eventually be used in trade and return to banks.

The policies advocated in this book come under the heading of limitation rather than of qualitative control. Qualitative control implies the enforcement of a given distribution of loans with a view to regulating economic activity. Limitation implies merely the enforcement of safety for the deposits of banks.

Further implications of a strict banking control by the Federal Reserve System have to do with control of economic activity in other lines. But the regulation of currency by the State has long been practiced, even at the height of the period of laissez faire. The prices of commodities have, until very recently, been determined by the market. Today, or at least until the year 1933, the prices of commodities have been regulated by the market except in cases where unequal bargaining power exists, as in public utility rates and wages for women and children. The elimination of a self regulating deposit banking system, which has failed to regulate itself, is rather an extension of the idea of a regulated currency than a forecast of the elimination of the self regulating markets for goods.

APPENDIX I

Indices of Seasonal Variation of Money Market Statistics

These indices are computed by the link relative method for the years 1919 through 1931, except as otherwise indicated.

	Amount of re-discounts at reserve banks	*Total bills and securities, Fed. reserve banks* *	*Bills bought in open market by Fed. reserve banks*	*Currency in circulation*
January	91.9	102.0	129.0	99.8
February	93.2	94.2	116.5	98.4
March	96.4	98.1	102.7	98.7
April	99.4	95.8	98.2	99.0
May	102.3	94.5	91.6	98.8
June	99.4	93.0	75.9	98.8
July	101.8	93.1	65.8	99.2
August	98.6	95.6	64.6	99.2
September	101.1	100.2	81.2	100.6
October	104.6	106.0	106.8	101.4
November	102.0	108.1	126.4	101.9
December	109.3	119.4	141.4	104.2

* From B. H. Beckhart, *The New York Money Market*, vol. ii.

LOANS OF REPORTING MEMBER BANKS

	Total loans	*Loans on securities for N. Y. C. banks* *	*All other loans, all reporting banks* *	*All other loans, banks outside N. Y. C.* *
January	100.7	103.1	98.7	99.2
February	99.0	99.3	98.2	98.8
March	99.8	98.2	99.8	99.5
April	99.7	98.9	100.1	99.6
May	99.5	99.2	99.8	99.5
June	98.7	101.6	99.5	99.5
July	99.5	100.4	99.7	99.6
August	99.3	97.3	100.1	99.8
September	100.2	98.6	101.3	100.5
October	101.3	99.8	101.4	101.7
November	101.1	100.4	101.1	101.1
December	101.2	102.2	100.3	101.2

* Computed for the period 1920-1931.

LOANS TO BROKERS AND LOANS TO CUSTOMERS OF BANKS ON SECURITY COLLATERAL

	Loans to brokers by N. Y. C. reporting member banks, all accounts *	*Loans to brokers by N. Y. C. reporting member banks, own account*	*Loans to brokers by N. Y. C. reporting member banks, account of out-of-town banks and others* †	*Loans directly to customers on securities*	
				By N. Y. C. reporting member banks ‡	*By reporting member banks outside N. Y. C.* ‡
Jan.	102.2	102.7	97.8	102.6	100.6
Feb.	101.3	98.6	101.9	99.5	98.3
Mar.	102.0	98.5	102.3	97.9	99.6
Apr.	101.1	97.8	102.1	98.3	98.8
May	100.5	98.4	102.0	98.7	98.2
June	99.7	104.7	97.7	99.3	100.0
July	98.1	102.7	98.1	99.7	101.0
Aug.	97.9	98.4	100.5	98.6	100.1
Sep.	99.4	98.5	99.8	99.8	100.0
Oct.	101.4	102.4	101.0	101.1	100.4
Nov.	98.1	96.8	101.0	101.0	101.0
Dec.	98.3	100.5	95.8	103.5	102.0

* From Haney, Logan and Gavens, *Brokers' Loans.*

† Computed from loans for the account of correspondents, 1919-1925 and loans for the account of out-of-town banks and others, 1926-1931.

‡ Computed for the period 1920-1931.

OTHER RELATED SERIES

	Due to banks by N. Y. C. reporting member banks *	*Call loan rates* †	*New corporate security issues*		
			All †	*Stocks* ‡	*Bonds and Notes*
Jan.	104.4	97.0	111.4	129.1	124.2
Feb.	101.3	103.8	95.5	109.5	105.8
Mar.	102.4	101.1	104.1	109.7	109.8
Apr.	101.4	101.2	116.3	121.8	120.0
May	98.1	99.3	116.4	141.9	112.4
June	99.0	99.8	99.7	107.0	110.1
July	101.8	95.5	73.5	69.4	93.1
Aug.	95.6	95.1	78.5	60.2	62.5
Sep.	97.0	99.8	98.7	66.8	88.3
Oct.	100.5	102.3	98.3	78.3	93.9
Nov.	99.8	99.7	98.1	88.4	83.1
Dec.	98.7	105.4	111.7	117.9	96.8

* Computed for the period April, 1920, through 1931.

† From Haney, Logan and Gavens, *Brokers' Loans*.

‡ The period, January through June, 1930, omitted from the computation.

BANKERS' ACCEPTANCES OUTSTANDING, END OF MONTH *

	Based on imports	*Based on exports*	*Based on domestic storage and shipment*	*Based on the creation of dollar exchange*	*Total outstanding*
Jan.	101.2	109.1	122.4	112.5	110.6
Feb.	102.2	108.1	106.8	106.7	107.1
Mar.	105.1	106.4	96.2	101.9	104.5
Apr.	104.9	100.6	98.8	98.5	100.5
May	101.5	96.9	91.8	99.5	97.2
June	99.4	91.7	83.2	90.9	93.5
July	96.6	88.4	79.6	87.3	89.5
Aug.	95.1	84.7	79.1	87.5	86.8
Sep.	96.8	89.1	84.8	101.2	91.0
Oct.	98.8	102.8	107.6	104.1	101.0
Nov.	98.6	110.7	122.5	104.7	106.8
Dec.	99.8	111.5	127.2	105.2	111.5

* Computed for the period 1925-1931. No defined seasonal for bankers' acceptances outstanding based on foreign storage and shipment.

BANKERS' ACCEPTANCES HELD BY FEDERAL RESERVE BANKS *

	Based on imports	*Based on exports*	*Based on foreign storage and shipment*	*Based on domestic storage and shipment*	*Based on the creation of dollar exchange*	*Payable in foreign currencies*	*Total held by federal reserve banks*
Jan. ...	109.0	120.8	113.6	123.2	125.1	†	110.0
Feb. ...	107.8	107.8	110.1	112.7	105.6	†	110.0
Mar. ..	113.0	105.9	99.9	103.7	101.4	†	110.2
Apr. ..	102.7	91.7	102.8	93.6	78.0	†	94.0
May ..	89.8	80.1	78.2	76.7	77.1	†	91.0
June ..	75.7	61.4	40.9	65.8	63.3	†	74.2
July ...	70.1	42.5	20.0	52.0	57.7	†	62.7
Aug. ..	83.5	50.3	45.6	59.0	75.1	†	74.9
Sep. ...	98.4	90.1	92.2	88.1	103.7	†	93.5
Oct. ...	112.0	138.4	154.3	126.6	129.4	†	118.5
Nov. ..	118.2	144.8	155.9	137.4	131.7	†	124.0
Dec. ..	119.8	166.2	186.5	161.2	151.9	†	137.0

* Computed for the period 1922-1931.

† No defined seasonal for bankers' acceptances payable in foreign currencies.

OTHER DATA USED IN THIS STUDY

	Amount of commercial paper outstanding, end of month	*Imports into the United States*	*Exports from the United States*
January	99.0	104.6	104.1
February	100.8	100.3	94.4
March	103.4	111.3	102.7
April	103.4	105.8	97.2
May	102.1	99.8	93.0
June	100.4	91.7	86.3
July	99.5	91.9	84.8
Aug.	99.9	93.5	91.2
Sep.	99.9	95.4	103.2
Oct.	99.9	104.0	120.6
Nov.	98.7	99.7	113.5
Dec.	93.0	102.0	109.0

APPENDIX II

The Reserve Position of Reporting Member Banks

Computed as follows: Vault cash plus reserves with Federal Reserve bank less borrowings from Federal Reserve bank as a percentage of total net deposits.

	1919	*1920*	*1921*	*1922*	*1923*	*1924*	*1925*
Jan.	3.25	0.13	—1.88	8.03	9.17	8.93	10.25
Feb.	1.62	—1.75	—1.83	8.97	8.61	9.09	9.60
March	1.34	—1.93	—1.46	9.80	8.35	9.47	9.38
April	1.52	—2.00	—0.25	10.07	8.29	9.35	9.31
May	1.25	—2.21	+1.25	10.57	8.10	9.82	9.50
June	2.38	—1.46	2.69	10.73	8.03	10.45	9.23
July	1.72	—1.64	3.10	10.60	7.50	10.56	9.07
Aug.	2.26	—2.42	4.02	10.45	7.57	10.65	8.65
Sept.	2.35	—2.63	4.84	10.20	7.34	10.70	8.37
Oct.	0.66	—3.41	5.32	9.86	7.17	10.44	8.20
Nov.	0.33	—3.48	6.31	8.77	7.72	10.41	8.35
Dec.	0.26	—3.17	6.79	8.90	7.95	10.37	8.21

	1926	*1927*	*1928*	*1929*	*1930*	*1931*	*1932*
Jan.	8.89	8.76	8:54	6.70	8.51	9.66	7.39
Feb.	8.59	8.90	8.21	6.53	8.85	9.39	7.02
March	8.43	8.71	7.94	6.04	9.13	9.48	7.74
April	8.65	8.64	7.48	5.95	9.20	9.43	8.84
May	8.82	8.55	6.64	6.26	9.30	9.64	10.25
June	9.03	8.87	5.85	6.26	9.34	9.67	9.92
July	8.68	8.64	5.56	5.79	9.39	9.77	9.67
Aug.	8.47	8.71	5.61	5.99	9.30	9.60	10.21
Sept.	8.15	8.67	5.66	6.19	9.38	9.52	11.07
Oct.	7.89	8.61	6.10	6.76	9.30	8.33	11.56
Nov.	8.04	8.74	6.42	7.02	9.26	7.81	11.90
Dec.	8.26	8.41	6.17	7.47	9.37	7.76	12.44

BIBLIOGRAPHY

Books

Beckhart, Benjamin Haggott, *Discount Policy of the Federal Reserve System*, New York, 1924.

Beckhart, Benjamin Haggott, ed., *The New York Money Market*, New York, 1931-1932, 4 vols.

Vol. I, *Origins and Development*, by Margaret G. Myers.

Vol. II, *Sources and Movements of Funds*, by B. H. Beckhart and James G. Smith.

Vol. III, *Uses of Funds*, by B. H. Beckhart.

Vol. IV, *External and Internal Relations*, by B. H. Beckhart, James G. Smith and William Adams Brown, Jr.

Burgess, W. Randolph, *The Reserve Banks and the Money Market*, New York, 1927.

Burgess, W. Randolph, ed., *Interpretations of Federal Reserve Policy in the Speeches and Writings of Benjamin Strong*, New York, 1930.

Harding, W. P. G., *The Formative Period of the Federal Reserve System*, New York, 1925.

Hardy, Charles O., *Credit Policies of the Federal Reserve System*, Washington, 1932.

Harris, S. E., *Twenty Years of Federal Reserve Policy*, Cambridge, 1933, 2 vols.

Reed, Harold L., *The Development of Federal Reserve Policy*, Boston and New York, 1922.

Federal Reserve Policy, 1921-1930, New York, 1931.

Riefler, Winfield W., *Money Rates and Money Markets in the United States*, New York, 1930.

Spahr, Walter E., *The Federal Reserve System and the Control of Credit*, New York, 1931.

Warburg, Paul M., *The Federal Reserve System*, New York, 1930, 2 vols.

Willis, H. Parker, *The Federal Reserve*, New York and Garden City, 1915.

The Federal Reserve System, New York, 1923.

Willis, H. Parker and Steiner, William H., *Federal Reserve Banking Practice*, New York, 1926.

Official Sources

United States Senate, Committee on Banking and Currency, *Hearings on H. R. 7837 (S. 2639)*, 63rd. Congress, 1st. Session, 1913, "A Bill to Provide for the Establishment of Federal Reserve Banks."

Hearings on S. Res. 113, 70th. Congress, 1st. Session, 1928, "A Resolution Favoring a Restriction of Loans by Federal Reserve Banks for Speculative Purposes."

Hearings of S. Res. 71, 71st. Congress, 3rd. Session, 1931, "To Make a Complete Survey of the National and Federal Reserve Banking Systems."

Hearings on S. Res. 4115, 72nd. Congress, 1st. Session, 1932, "A Bill to Provide for the Safer and More Effective Use of the Assets of Federal Reserve Banks and of National Banking Associations, to Regulate Interbank Control, to Prevent the Undue Diversion of Funds into Speculative Operations, and for Other Purposes."

United States House of Representatives, Committee on Banking and Currency, *Hearings on H. R. 7895*, 69th. Congress, 1st. Session, 1926, "A Bill to Amend Paragraph (d) of Section 14 of the Federal Reserve Act, as Amended, to Provide for the Stabilization of the Price Level for Commodities in General."

Hearings on H. R. 11806, 71st. Congress, 1st. Session, 1928, "A Bill to Amend the Act Approved December 23, 1913, Known as the Federal Reserve Act; to Define Certain Policies Toward Which the Powers of the Federal Reserve System Shall be Directed; to Further Promote the Maintenance of a Stable Gold Standard; to Promote the Stability of Commerce, Industry, Agriculture, and Employment; to Assist in Realizing a More Stable Purchasing Power of the Dollar; and for Other Purposes."

Federal Reserve Board, *Annual Reports.*

Digest of Rulings of the Federal Reserve Board, 1914–1923.

Federal Reserve Bulletin.

Reports of Federal Reserve Agents to the Federal Reserve Board.

United States Comptroller of the Currency, *Annual Reports.*

Commercial and Financial Chronicle.

American Acceptance Council, *Acceptance Bulletin.*

Standard Statistics Co., *Statistical Bulletin.*

United States Department of Commerce, *Survey of Current Business.*

INDEX

Bei Fragen zur Produktsicherheit wenden Sie sich bitte an:
If you have any questions regarding product safety,
please contact:

Walter de Gruyter GmbH
Genthiner Straße 13
10785 Berlin
productsafety@degruyterbrill.com